PSYCH QUEST

A GAMER'S INTRO TO PSYCHOLOGY

ROTEM (LEV) LEVIM

THANKS

This couldn't have been done without my family and friends. I would specifically like to thank Omer Ackerman, Menny Barzilay, Nadav Ginosar, Dean Movshovitz, Ran Goren, Eran Palmon, Mor Epel, my family and the Snyders! Love you all!

TABLE OF CONTENTS

PREFACE

THE MOTIVATION BEHIND THIS BOOK

As someone who has dealt with depression, I've recently consulted with a friend who gave me great advice for when times are tough. He put it in Gamer terms... and, as I'm a gamer... it blew my mind. I began to think about everything in this way. It has freed me almost instantly from moments I've felt down. I feel blessed and wanted to share this idea with as many Gamers as possible so they can benefit from it too.

THE MAIN IDEA

As soon as you feel down, think of yourself as a video game character—one who spawned to this exact moment, given the exact problem and skill set that you have now. Now, think about the ultimate goal that your character has. What must the character endure to reach that goal? How can they better themselves to reach it in the best manner? What is your strategy to make the character win the game? Now, do just that.

THIS BOOK

In this book, I want to demonstrate this philosophy, show different game heroes' storylines, and analyze them using different psychological models. Embark on a captivating journey through the realms of psychology and gaming. Delve into the intricate minds of your favorite video game characters through various psychological models to dissect their motivations, behaviors, and intricacies. Unveiling the psychological underpinnings that drive characters, the book serves as a fascinating exploration of human nature through the lens of gaming narratives. A unique blend of entertainment and education, readers will find themselves immersed in a rich tapestry of psychological concepts, making it an ideal resource for those seeking to grasp the basics of "Intro to Psychology" through the compelling narratives of beloved gaming icons. Get ready to unlock the secrets of the virtual psyche and gain a deeper understanding of psychology and Video Game characters that have captured our hearts.

Let's-a go!

GAMER TYPES

In online multiplayer games, Richard Bartle's model unveils a fascinating tapestry of player motivations, neatly categorizing them into four distinct archetypes.

- First are the **Achievers**, creatures of ambition fueled by the relentless pursuit of in-game glory. They savor each point, relish climbing up levels, and cherish rare artifacts like prized trophies. The Achievers wear competitiveness as their armor, finding solace in the sweet taste of accomplishment and the spotlight it brings.

- Then there are the **Explorers**, wanderers of the digital frontier, whose purpose transcends competition or reward. Their quest is one of curiosity, a journey to peel back the layers of virtual landscapes. These individuals crave discovery like a fine wine, uncovering hidden gems, easter eggs, and the subtle dance of game mechanics.

- In another corner, we encounter the **Socializers**. These souls thrive on the human connections forged amid the gaming universe. For them, the game's true essence lies in camaraderie, group exploits, and the rich tapestry of in-game conversations. Here, it's not about achievements or uncharted territories; it's about building a vibrant digital community.

- Then, there are the **Killers**, masters of conflict who revel in the thrill of competition. These players wield skills like weapons, seeking dominance and the intoxicating power it bestows. It's not just about winning; it's about the visceral impact they have on other players' experiences.

Most players shift between these motivations, their preferences ebbing and flowing with the tides of mood and game choice. This model is a framework mainly used to understand player behaviours and help game designers create games that engage different players. Now, Let's think of life as an online multiplayer game. How will you navigate your character to receive the most joy, success, and respect? How do you define each of these? Don't just stumble through the game. Create a strategy. Create a life plan.

DISCLAIMER #1

It's essential to remember that the characters are fictional characters designed to be relatable, likable, and heroic. The traits and psychology attributed to them are carefully crafted to make them endearing and iconic characters in the gaming world. While their experiences and adventures may have influenced certain aspects of their personality, ultimately, the character's psychology reflects the creators' intent to create a character that resonates with players and embodies the spirit of heroism and adventure.

DISCLAIMER #2

The psychological analysis of characters presented herein is purely speculative and conducted solely for artistic and entertainment purposes. The creator of this analysis holds no professional licenses or qualifications in psychology, therapy, or any related field. The interpretations provided are subjective and should not be considered accurate depictions of the characters' mental states or personalities. It is crucial to understand that any attempt to analyze individuals, including fictional characters, without proper training and qualifications may lead to inaccurate or misleading conclusions. This analysis should not be used as a substitute for professional psychological advice, diagnosis, or treatment. I acknowledge the limitations of my understanding and emphasize that the interpretations offered are not to be considered authoritative or definitive. If any information provided is found to be incorrect or potentially harmful, it is purely unintentional, and the creator apologizes for any discrepancies. Readers are encouraged to seek professional guidance for any mental health concerns and should not rely on the content presented here for therapeutic purposes.

DISCLAIMER #3
There may be spoilers! So.. Spoiler Alert!

MARIO

Let's start off with Mario, one of the most iconic characters - brought to us by Nintendo. Generally, Mario's quest revolves around saving Princess Peach, ruler of the Mushroom Kingdom, from the evil Bowser. In the early days, Mario started as a humble carpenter named Jumpman in "Donkey Kong," where he had to rescue his girlfriend, Lady, from Donkey Kong himself. Later on, in Super Mario Bros., he had to save Princess Peach alongside his brother Luigi. They embark on a journey through various worlds, overcoming obstacles, defeating enemies and collecting power-ups to ultimately face Bowser. Mario teams up with many other notable allies like Toad, Yoshi and Princess Daisy in various installments and spin-off series. He has multiple abilities and power-ups to overcome obstacles like the enlarging Super Mushroom, Fireballs from the Fire Flower and being temporarily invincible with the Super Star.

CHALLENGES

Mario has faced a wide array of challenges and obstacles throughout his adventures:

- Enemies and Boss Battles: From Goombas and Koopa Troopas to more formidable foes like Bowser. These enemies often obstruct his path and require strategic jumping or the use of power-ups to defeat.

- Platforming: Mario must navigate through intricate levels filled with moving platforms, bottomless pits, spikes, and other hazards. Precision jumping and timing are essential to progress through the puzzles and traps.
- Power-Up Management: Mario often gains access to various power-ups like Super Mushrooms, Fire Flowers, and SuperStars. Managing these power-ups and deciding when to use them is crucial, as they provide temporary advantages and can help Mario overcome specific challenges.
- Underwater and Flying Sections: Sometimes, Mario has to go through underwater levels with reduced mobility and breathing limitations. There are also flying sections, such as those involving the Super Leaf or Wing Cap, introducing unique challenges in his movement.
- Timed Challenges: Time-based challenges, where Mario must complete a mission or objective within a strict time limit, add an element of urgency. Failure to meet the time requirements often results in the loss of a life.
- Environmental Hazards: Mario must contend with many environmental hazards, including lava, quicksand, ice, poisoned water, and more. These hazards can instantly defeat him, so he must navigate carefully.
- Maze-Like Areas: Some parts of his journey are like intricate mazes, where he must find keys, unlock doors, and explore multiple pathways to reach the goal. These can be particularly challenging in terms of navigation.
- Gravity and Physics Manipulation: Sometimes, Mario faces unique challenges due to gravity manipulation and planetary physics. Mario must adapt to shifting environments and navigate celestial bodies.

PSYCHOLOGY

Mario's character displays psychological traits that reflect his experiences and the challenges he faces. We can analyze how these hardships might affect his psychology:

- Resilience: Mario's repeated encounters with challenging enemies, obstacles, and life-threatening situations likely contribute to his resilience. He doesn't give up easily and continues to pursue his goals despite setbacks. This resilience can be seen as a reflection of his determination and mental fortitude.

- Problem-Solving Skills: Mario's adventures often require thinking quickly and finding creative solutions to complex puzzles and obstacles. This constant problem-solving can lead to the development of strong cognitive skills and adaptability.
- Courage and Confidence: Facing dangerous enemies and overcoming treacherous environments would likely boost Mario's courage and self-confidence. Successfully conquering these challenges can reinforce his belief in his abilities.
- Empathy and Altruism: Mario's willingness to risk his own safety to rescue Princess Peach and protect the Mushroom Kingdom demonstrates a strong sense of empathy and altruism. These experiences could reinforce his values of helping others and doing what is right.
- Social Bonds: Mario's close relationships with characters like Luigi, Toad, and Yoshi are likely strengthened by shared experiences and challenges. These bonds provide him with emotional support and a sense of belonging, contributing to his overall psychological well-being.
- Adaptability: Mario's encounters with various power-ups, environments, and enemies require him to adapt quickly to changing circumstances. This adaptability could translate into a willingness to embrace change and take on new challenges in his life.
- Optimism: Despite adversity, Mario's upbeat and positive attitude suggests a natural optimism. This outlook on life can be a coping mechanism for dealing with the constant challenges he encounters.
- Moral Code: Mario consistently acts in a morally upright manner, which could indicate that his experiences have reinforced a strong sense of ethics and integrity.
- Motivation: The challenges he faces, particularly in his quest to rescue Princess Peach, provide Mario with a clear and motivating purpose. This sense of purpose and mission can contribute to his psychological well-being.

MASLOW'S HIERARCHY OF NEEDS & MARIO

One psychological model that could be applied to understanding Mario's behavior is Abraham Maslow's Hierarchy of Needs. This model presents a hierarchy of human needs that individuals strive to fulfill, ranging from basic physiological to higher-level psychological needs. It is theorized that a person needs to meet the basic needs at the bottom of the pyramid before moving on to fulfilling other needs. Let's explore how this model could be applied to Mario:

- Physiological Needs: At the base of the pyramid are the most basic physiological needs necessary for survival, such as food, water, shelter, and sleep. These needs must be satisfied before an individual can move on to addressing higher-level needs. Mario usually has a bar or "lives" to show his power level. If attacked, Mario either loses a life or has less power to continue his mission without recharging. This aligns with fulfilling his basic physiological need for sustenance and survival. In his adventures, Mario seeks to ensure that the Mushroom Kingdom's stability is preserved, addressing the foundational needs for himself and others.

- Safety Needs: Once physiological needs are met, people seek safety and security. This includes physical safety, financial stability, health, and protection from harm or danger. Mario frequently confronts dangerous situations and enemies, showcasing his role as a protector of the Mushroom Kingdom. His actions align with fulfilling the safety needs, not only for himself but also for his friends and the citizens of the kingdom. He faces risks to ensure the safety of others, demonstrating a commitment to this level of the hierarchy.

- Love and Belongingness Needs: After safety needs are satisfied, individuals seek social connections, love, and a sense of belonging. This includes relationships with family, friends, romantic partners, and a desire to be part of social groups or communities. Throughout his adventures, Mario forms strong bonds with his friends and allies, such as Luigi, Toad, and Yoshi. He cooperates and demonstrates a sense of belongingness within these relationships. This reflects his pursuit of love and companionship, meeting the psychological need for social connections.

- Esteem Needs: These involve the desire for self-esteem and the esteem of others. This includes self-respect, confidence, achievement, recognition, and respect from others. Fulfillment of these needs contributes to feelings of self-worth. While Mario is humble, his reputation as a heroic figure and savior of the Mushroom Kingdom does bring him a certain level of esteem. He is respected and admired by his peers and the citizens he protects. His consistent acts of bravery and heroism contribute to fulfilling his esteem needs, garnering recognition and admiration from others.
- Self-Actualization: At the pinnacle of the pyramid is self-actualization, representing the realization of one's full potential and personal growth. This level includes creativity, problem-solving, self-expression, and a deep sense of fulfillment and purpose. Mario's adventures and constant striving to overcome challenges could be seen as a pursuit of self-actualization. His ability to adapt, solve problems, and face adversity suggests that he is driven by a desire to reach his fullest potential.
- Self-Transcendence (Beyond Maslow's Model) - While not a part of Maslow's original hierarchy, some modern interpretations of psychological needs include self-transcendence, which involves focusing on goals beyond oneself. Mario's selflessness in repeatedly rescuing Princess Peach and protecting the Mushroom Kingdom could be seen as a form of self-transcendence, where his actions extend beyond personal needs and desires.

The Hierarchy of Needs is often used in psychology and other fields to understand human motivation, behavior, and well-being. It highlights the idea that individuals strive for personal growth and self-fulfillment once their more fundamental needs are met. Maslow's theory suggests that individuals typically progress through these levels sequentially, with lower-level needs taking precedence over higher-level ones. However, it's important to note that not everyone follows this exact sequence, and individual experiences can vary.

THE LEGEND OF ZELDA

The Legend of Zelda (Nintendo) features Link, not Zelda. Zelda is the name of the princess whom Link is often tasked with rescuing. Link often also needs to stop Ganon, also known as Ganondorf. He's a courageous young hero, often dressed in green attire and wielding a sword and shield, chosen by destiny to become the hero of Hyrule. He embarks on a quest to obtain the Triforce, a powerful artifact or some other magical item to thwart Ganon's evil plans. He is known for his combat skills and ability to wield various weapons, including swords, bows, boomerangs, and magical items. Throughout his adventures, he gains new abilities and equipment to help him overcome obstacles and enemies. His journey involves exploring a vast and often magical world, solving puzzles, battling enemies, and collecting items to aid him in his quest. He interacts with others who provide guidance, information, and assistance along the way. Link's specific tasks and challenges can vary widely, but his ultimate goal remains consistent: to defeat the forces of darkness, rescue Princess Zelda, and restore peace to the land of Hyrule.

CHALLENGES

Link faces a wide range of challenges throughout his adventures:

- Dungeons and Puzzles: To advance, he must solve intricate puzzles, defeat powerful bosses, and navigate through dungeons to collect important items.

- Combat: He often encounters various enemies, from simple creatures to formidable bosses, which require skill and strategy and he must use his weapons and abilities effectively to defeat these foes.
- Environmental Hazards: He journeys through environmental hazards like lava, quicksand, and bottomless pits. He must figure out how to navigate these hazards safely, often using special items or abilities.
- Time-Based Challenges: He may need to complete certain tasks within a limited timeframe or race against the clock to prevent a catastrophe. This creates immense time pressure.
- Navigation and Exploration: He must explore different regions, solve riddles, and navigate through forests, mountains, deserts, and underwater areas.
- Moral and Ethical Choices: Sometimes, Link is presented with moral and ethical dilemmas that can lead to different outcomes, adding meaning to his decisions.
- Emotional Challenges: He often faces emotional challenges as he witnesses the consequences of Ganon's actions when he tries to rescue Princess Zelda.

Overall, Link's journey is filled with a series of demanding trials that test his physical abilities, intelligence, resourcefulness, and moral character.

PSYCHOLOGY

While Link is usually silent, there are some general themes and interpretations regarding how the hardships he faces might affect him:

- Resilience: Link's repeated exposure to challenging situations and his ability to overcome them can be seen as a testament to his resilience. He is determined to succeed in his quest, even when facing overwhelming odds.
- Courage: Courage is central, and Link's willingness to confront danger and face his fears head-on exemplifies this. His courage grows as he progresses through his adventures, and he often inspires others with his bravery.
- Isolation: His role as a hero often requires him to work alone, without much emotional support or guidance. This isolation may lead to feelings of loneliness or solitude. This sense of isolation

could impact him profoundly, making him a somewhat enigmatic and solitary figure.

- Trauma: Link may experience some level of psychological trauma. He witnesses the destruction of his homeland, battles powerful foes, and often experiences the loss of friends or allies.
- Responsibility: In many of his adventures, he carries the weight of the world on his shoulders, as he is often the only one who can stop Ganon or other threats to Hyrule. This sense of responsibility may lead to feelings of pressure and the need to prove himself constantly, which could impact his mental health.

ERIKSON'S PSYCHOSOCIAL STAGES & LINK

Erik Erikson's psychosocial stages of development can provide a valuable framework for analyzing Link's character growth and psychological development throughout the Legend of Zelda series. Erikson was a prominent psychologist known for his theory of psychosocial development. His model consists of eight stages, each representing a different developmental challenge that individuals face throughout their lives. The main point of Erikson's model is that successfully resolving each stage's challenge contributes to healthy psychosocial development, while failure to do so can lead to psychological and social difficulties. Erikson believed that individuals go through these stages from infancy to old age and that each stage involves a unique conflict or crisis that must be resolved. Here's an analysis of Link through Erikson's model:

- Trust vs. Mistrust (Infancy): In this stage, infants develop a sense of trust or mistrust based on their caregivers' reliability and responsiveness to their needs. Link's earliest experiences might be harder to pinpoint due to the nature of the series. However, he starts his journey as a young, inexperienced hero. The challenges he faces, such as overcoming self-doubt and uncertainty, could be seen as reflections of the trust vs. mistrust conflict. His success in these early challenges helps shape his sense of competence and trust in his abilities.
- Autonomy vs. Shame and Doubt (Early Childhood): Toddlers seek to assert their independence and control over their actions, leading to feelings of autonomy or self-doubt if their efforts are met with criticism or restriction. Link's growth into a more capable hero reflects his struggle with autonomy and self-

control. His ability to master new skills, solve puzzles, and overcome obstacles can contribute to his sense of independence and self-confidence. Failures or setbacks, on the other hand, might trigger feelings of shame and doubt.

- Initiative vs. Guilt (Preschool Age): Young children explore their environment and take initiative in tasks, fostering a sense of purpose, confidence, or potential guilt if their actions are discouraged. Link's proactive approach to helping others and taking on quests aligns with the initiative vs. guilt stage. His willingness to engage in challenges and take responsibility for the well-being of Hyrule showcases his developing sense of purpose and contribution to the world.

- Industry vs. Inferiority (School Age): School-age children strive to master new skills and tasks, contributing to a sense of competence and industry or feelings of inadequacy and inferiority if they perceive themselves as incapable. Link's progression through various dungeons, temples, and quests can be seen as him striving to master his environment and develop industry. His ability to successfully complete tasks and overcome obstacles contributes to his feelings of competence and accomplishment. Failures or perceived shortcomings might lead to feelings of inferiority.

- Identity vs. Role Confusion (Adolescence): Adolescents navigate their identity development, forming a coherent sense of self or experiencing confusion and uncertainty about their roles and values. Link's journey to discover his role as the hero and his connection to the Triforce could align with the identity vs. role confusion stage. His exploration of his destiny and self-identity can lead to personal growth and a clearer sense of purpose.

- Intimacy vs. Isolation (Young Adulthood): Young adults seek to form close, meaningful relationships and establish intimacy while avoiding social isolation and loneliness. The relationships Link forms with characters like Princess Zelda, companions, and allies can be analyzed within the context of intimacy vs. isolation. His ability to build connections and trust with others contributes to his emotional growth and capacity for intimacy.

- Generativity vs. Stagnation (Middle Adulthood): Middle-aged adults find purpose in contributing to the well-being of others and society, experiencing generativity, or may feel unproductive and stagnant if they lack meaningful accomplishments. While Link's age is typically depicted as young, his actions of protecting and preserving the land of Hyrule could symbolize generativity. His willingness to sacrifice for the greater good and ensure the well-being of future generations aligns with this stage.

- Ego Integrity vs. Despair (Late Adulthood): In later life, individuals reflect on their achievements and find a sense of satisfaction and integrity. Alternatively, they may face feelings of regret and despair if they perceive their lives as unfulfilled. As Link's journey continues, he might face challenges that force him to reflect on his life's accomplishments and the legacy he leaves behind. The resolution of his quests and his impact on Hyrule's future could contribute to his sense of ego integrity.

Analyzing Link through Erikson's model can provide insights into how his character evolves, faces challenges, and matures throughout his heroic journey.

WHAT CAN WE LEARN?

Link goes through many challenges throughout his journey. He must think creatively, explore thoroughly and adapt to the unique challenges presented. He decides to persevere with determination, even when facing overwhelming odds. His purpose and commitment drives him forward and inspires others. His actions speak louder than words. Link's journey is not just physical but also one of personal growth and self-discovery. As he overcomes challenges and acquires new abilities, he matures as a character.

PORTAL

In Portal (Valve Corporation, 2007), Chell, a human test subject, finds herself trapped in the Aperture Science Enrichment Center, a mysterious and seemingly abandoned research facility. She is silent and has no voice throughout her journey. She is unaware of how she ended up there, and her backstory is not explicitly revealed. While Chell doesn't have a voiced personality, her actions and perseverance convey her determination to escape the testing facility. She goes through a series of increasingly complex and mind-bending puzzle chambers, all while dealing with the manipulative AI GLaDOS (Genetic Lifeform and Disk Operating System). As she progresses through the Aperture Science Enrichment Center, she becomes the focal point of GLaDOS' sinister experiments. GLaDOS toys with her emotions and tries to hinder her progress. The story and relationship between Chell and GLaDOS unfold as the journey progresses.

CHALLENGES

Chell faces a series of challenging and sometimes perilous situations as she navigates through the Aperture Science Enrichment Center.

- Solving Complex Puzzles: Chell's main journey revolves around solving various intricate puzzles using the Portal Gun. Each test chamber presents different obstacles and physics-based challenges that require creative thinking and quick reflexes to overcome.

- Dealing with GLaDOS: Chell's primary antagonist is GLaDOS, the AI that controls the Aperture Science facility. GLaDOS initially appears to be a friendly and helpful guide, but her true, malevolent intentions become apparent as she progresses. She subjects Chell to dangerous tests and lies and manipulates her emotions, making her journey even more treacherous.
- Escaping Lethal Hazards: The testing facility is filled with hazardous materials, such as deadly energy pellets, crushing platforms, and pools of toxic goo. Chell must navigate these dangerous elements while focusing on solving the puzzles.
- Enduring Psychological Tests: GLaDOS' mind games extend beyond the physical puzzles. Chell is subjected to psychological tests that aim to provoke emotional responses. GLaDOS taunts and mocks her throughout, trying to break her spirit.
- Discovering the Truth: As Chell progresses, she uncovers hidden rooms and hidden messages left behind by previous test subjects. These hints provide subtle clues about Aperture Science's dark history and GLaDOS' past actions.
- Escaping Fire: Towards the latter part of her journey, Chell finds herself in life-threatening situations where she must outrun a spreading fire that engulfs parts of the facility. This adds a time-sensitive element to the challenges she faces.
- Confronting GLaDOS: As Chell nears the end of her journey, she faces a final confrontation with GLaDOS. This epic battle involves using the Portal Gun strategically to defeat the AI and escape the facility.

PSYCHOLOGY

Chell's journey in Portal is not just about physical tests but also about her resilience and determination to survive and escape the treacherous facility. Going through the Aperture Science Enrichment Center undoubtedly has a profound influence on her. The experiences she goes through in her journey shape her mental and emotional state in several ways:

- Resilience and Determination: Chell's relentless pursuit of escape from the testing facility showcases her resilience and determination. Despite facing numerous challenges, dangerous obstacles, and GLaDOS' manipulations, she keeps pushing forward.

- Critical Thinking and Problem-Solving Skills: The puzzles and tests Chell encounters require creative and critical thinking to solve. As she progresses, she becomes more adept at understanding the physics of the Portal Gun and applying it in novel ways. This enhances her problem-solving skills and adaptability.
- Emotional Endurance: Throughout her journey, Chell is subjected to GLaDOS' taunts, manipulations, and psychological tests. Her ability to endure these emotional trials without breaking down or succumbing to despair shows her emotional strength and self-control.
- Cautious Trust: Chell starts with a degree of trust in GLaDOS, believing she's there to help her. However, as the AI's true intentions become apparent, Chell becomes more cautious and skeptical. This experience likely influences her ability to trust others in the future, especially those in positions of authority or power.
- Curiosity and Exploration: As Chell discovers hidden rooms and messages throughout the facility, her curiosity is piqued, and she becomes more willing to explore and investigate her surroundings. This newfound curiosity may lead her to seek answers and question the world around her in other situations.
- Isolation and Solitude: Chell's isolation within the testing facility and her lack of direct communication with others contribute to a sense of solitude. Spending an extended period without human interaction can affect one's psyche, potentially leading to feelings of loneliness or detachment.
- Empowerment and Self-Efficacy: As Chell overcomes each challenge, she gains a sense of empowerment and self-efficacy— the belief in her ability to accomplish tasks and influence her environment. This growing confidence could positively impact her self-esteem and approach to future challenges.

SELF-DETERMINATION THEORY & CHELL

Self-Determination Theory (SDT) is a psychological framework developed by Deci and Ryan in the 1980s that focuses on the motivation behind human behavior and the conditions that support or hinder it. It is widely used in fields such as psychology, education, and sports to understand why people do what they do. SDT posits that individuals have innate psychological needs that, when satisfied, promote well-being and optimal functioning. Here are the basics of Self-Determination Theory and how Chell can be examined through this framework:

First off, there are three Basic Psychological Needs:

- Autonomy: Autonomy refers to the need to feel in control of one's own actions and choices. It involves a sense of self-direction and the ability to make decisions that align with one's values and interests. Chell's quest for escape from the testing facility reflects her pursuit of autonomy and freedom. Despite GLaDOS' control and manipulation, Chell's actions demonstrate her desire to assert her autonomy and make her own choices.

- Competence: Competence is the need to feel effective and capable in one's actions. It involves a sense of mastery, accomplishment, and the belief that one can successfully handle tasks and challenges. Chell's progression through the puzzles in the facility highlights her need for competence. As she solves increasingly complex challenges, she gains a sense of mastery and achievement, fulfilling her need for competence and self-efficacy.

- Relatedness: Relatedness pertains to the need for social connections and a sense of belonging. It involves feeling connected to others, experiencing caring relationships, and feeling understood and valued by others. While Chell lacks direct human interaction, her interactions with GLaDOS and the snippets of past test subjects' experiences satisfy her need for relatedness, albeit in a distorted way. Her exploration of hidden messages and her connection to previous characters showcase her attempt to establish some form of social connection.

There are also two Types of Motivation:

- Intrinsic Motivation: Intrinsic motivation occurs when individuals engage in an activity because they find it inherently interesting, enjoyable, or personally meaningful. They are driven by internal factors, such as curiosity or passion. If Chell was interested in solving these puzzles out of curiosity (and not to try to escape death), it would be intrinsic.

- Extrinsic Motivation: Extrinsic motivation involves engaging in an activity for external rewards or to avoid punishments. This type of motivation can vary in terms of its autonomy-supportive or controlling nature. We can see that Chell's motivation is very Extrinsic as she tries to escape the facility and avoid death.

SDT suggests that motivation exists on a continuum, ranging from low autonomy (controlled motivation) to high autonomy (intrinsic motivation). The most self-determined motivation occurs when individuals engage in activities because they genuinely value them and have a sense of choice. This theory also takes into account environments and autonomy.

- Supportive vs. Controlling Environments: SDT emphasizes the importance of creating environments that support individuals' autonomy, competence, and relatedness needs. Supportive environments facilitate more self-determined motivation while controlling environments can undermine it. In Portal, The Aperture Science facility, controlled by GLaDOS, is initially a highly controlling environment. As Chell progresses, she navigates this environment to regain control and autonomy. The Portal Gun itself is a tool that enhances Chell's autonomy, enabling her to create portals and solve puzzles in her own way.
- Autonomy Supportive Practices: To promote self-determination, practitioners can use autonomy-supportive strategies, such as offering choice, providing opportunities for skill development, offering constructive feedback, and acknowledging individuals' perspectives and feelings. Research has shown that when individuals' basic psychological needs are satisfied, they are more likely to experience greater well-being, engagement, and persistence in their activities. It can lead to improved performance, greater satisfaction, and a sense of fulfillment. Chell's psychological well-being is likely affected by the constant challenges, isolation, and manipulations by GLaDOS. However, her determination to overcome these challenges and regain control aligns with the idea that satisfying basic psychological needs contributes to well-being.

This theory has been applied to many domains, including education, workplace, sports, healthcare and personal development. It provided a framework for understanding how to foster motivation and well-being. Chell's resilience demonstrates her ability to cope with adversity and not give up, even in seemingly hopeless situations. Even in the hardest times, she pushes forward with emotional strength and self-control while enhancing her problem-solving skills and adaptability. Chell's journey is a testament to the human capacity for resilience, adaptability, and personal growth, even in the face of daunting circumstances.

HALF LIFE

The main character of the Half-Life series is Dr. Gordon Freeman. He is a theoretical physicist who works at the fictional Black Mesa Research Facility, a top-secret research facility in New Mexico, USA. An unforeseen resonance cascade occurs during an experiment involving a strange crystalline substance called "Xen" and an anti-mass spectrometer, resulting in a dimensional rift that brings alien creatures into the facility. Freeman must fight through the facility, battling alien creatures and military personnel sent to contain the situation. As he progresses, he discovers that the facility's management is attempting to cover up the incident. Ten years later, Earth is under the control of the Combine, a powerful alien empire that invaded after the resonance cascade. The enigmatic G-Man brings Gordon Freeman out of stasis and joins a group of rebels led by scientist Eli Vance and his daughter Alyx. Together, they work to fight against the Combine's occupation of Earth. Later, they try to escape City 17 and deliver important information to other resistance groups.

CHALLENGES

Freeman faces a series of significant challenges and obstacles throughout the Half-Life series as he tries to navigate the dangerous and chaotic events at the Black Mesa Research Facility and beyond.

- Alien Threats: The accident at Black Mesa opens rifts to other dimensions, allowing various hostile alien creatures to invade the facility. Gordon must battle these alien beings, including headcrabs, vortigaunts, and the formidable Nihilanth.
- Government Agents: As the situation at Black Mesa spirals out of control, the U.S. government sends in special forces to contain and eliminate any witnesses. These government agents, known as the Hazardous Environment Combat Unit (HECU), become another formidable adversary for Gordon.
- Environmental Hazards: Black Mesa is a vast and complex facility with numerous environmental hazards, such as toxic waste, electrified areas, and precarious ledges. Gordon must navigate these hazards under fire from aliens and government agents.
- Obstacles: Freeman has to figure out how to go through various obstacles and locked doors. He often needs to find keys, manipulate machinery, and use physics-based solutions to overcome these challenges.
- Isolation: Gordon Freeman is often alone in his journey, adding to the sense of isolation and vulnerability.
- Loss of Allies: Throughout the series, Gordon loses allies and friends, which adds emotional weight to the story.
- Time Pressure: As the situation at Black Mesa and later in City 17 worsens, there is often a sense of urgency. Gordon must act quickly to achieve his objectives and evade pursuers.
- The G-Man: A mysterious character known as the G-Man appears at various points. He seems to have control over Gordon's fate and presents enigmatic challenges and choices to Gordon, adding an extra layer of intrigue and uncertainty.

Freeman's journey is a test of survival, resourcefulness, and determination as he confronts different obstacles and tries to uncover the truth behind the Black Mesa incident and the ensuing consequences.

PSYCHOLOGY

The challenges that Freeman has to overcome test his intellect, combat skills, and resilience with a tad of underlying psychological issues:

- Isolation and Loneliness: Freeman is a silent protagonist, meaning he doesn't engage in direct verbal communication. This could lead to a sense of isolation and loneliness, as he lacks the ability to express his thoughts, emotions, or concerns to others. He navigates the world largely in silence, which might make him feel disconnected from those around him.

- Survivor's Guilt: He is one of the few survivors of the catastrophic events at Black Mesa. Witnessing the death and suffering of colleagues and friends during the resonance cascade could lead to survivor's guilt, a psychological challenge where he might grapple with feelings of responsibility and remorse for surviving when others did not.
- Existential Crisis: The Half-Life series introduces existential questions about the meaning of Freeman's actions and the larger purpose in a world overrun by alien forces and oppressive governments. He might face existential crises, struggling to find meaning and purpose in a world where humanity is under constant threat.
- Emotional Suppression: Freeman's stoic and silent demeanor could be indicative of emotional suppression. He may keep his emotions in check as a coping mechanism, particularly when faced with overwhelming situations and the need to remain focused on survival.
- Constant Stress and Uncertainty: The continuous high-stress environments, uncertain future, and unresolved cliffhangers throughout his journey could contribute to chronic stress and anxiety. Freeman must constantly be vigilant, adapt to changing circumstances, and navigate unpredictable challenges.
- Identity and Self-Reflection: The lack of communication and introspection by the character can raise questions about his sense of identity and self. Freeman might grapple with questions about who he is and what he represents in a world filled with extraordinary events and powerful forces.
- Moral Dilemmas: Freeman often faces moral dilemmas, such as whether to engage in violent conflict, make difficult decisions about the fate of certain characters or groups, or choose between personal survival and the greater good. These moral challenges could weigh heavily on his psyche.
- Post-Traumatic Stress: Given the traumatic events he witnesses and the constant threat of danger, Freeman may experience symptoms of post-traumatic stress disorder (PTSD), including flashbacks, hypervigilance, and emotional numbing.

Freeman's mentality is likely influenced by a mix of trauma, resilience, empowerment, uncertainty, and adaptability.

THE TRANSACTIONAL MODEL OF STRESS AND COPING & FREEMAN

Richard Lazarus, a prominent psychologist, is known for his work on stress and coping. He developed a comprehensive model focusing on the cognitive and emotional processes involved in dealing with stressors. Here are the key components of Lazarus's model and how they can be applied to Gordan Freeman:

- Stressor: In this model, a stressor is an external event or circumstance perceived as challenging or threatening. Stressors can take various forms, such as a difficult task, a conflict, or a major life change.
- Primary Appraisal: The first step in Lazarus's model is the primary appraisal, where an individual evaluates the significance of a stressor. This involves determining whether the stressor is irrelevant, potentially beneficial, or stressful. If the stressor is deemed stressful, it leads to the next step.
- Secondary Appraisal: After identifying a potentially stressful stressor, individuals engage in secondary appraisal. This involves assessing their available resources, including their coping abilities, social support, and other factors that can help them deal with the stressor.
- Coping: Coping strategies are the efforts made to manage or reduce the stress caused by the identified stressor. Lazarus categorized coping strategies into two main types:
  - Problem-Focused Coping: This involves taking action to address the stressor directly. For example, if a person is stressed about an upcoming exam, problem-focused coping might involve studying more, seeking help from a tutor, or creating a study schedule.

    A. Adaptability and Resourcefulness - Freeman makes use of available tools and weapons to navigate through hazardous environments and combat alien threats. His ability to think on his feet and find solutions to immediate challenges showcases his problem-solving skills.

  B. Resistance Against Oppression - Freeman joins the resistance movement to actively fight against the Combine's oppressive rule. His decision to participate in the resistance demonstrates his determination to tackle the underlying problem of alien occupation.

  C. Leadership and Initiative - Freeman often takes the lead in dire situations, guiding others and making crucial decisions. This shows his willingness to step up and take action when needed.

- Emotion-Focused Coping: This involves managing the emotional response to the stressor. It may include strategies like seeking emotional support from friends, engaging in relaxation techniques, or using positive self-talk to reduce emotional distress.

  A. Internalization of Emotions: Freeman's emotional state is not explicitly communicated to others. This internalization of emotions might reflect his tendency to keep his feelings to himself, even in the face of significant challenges.

  B. Resilience and Determination: Freeman's consistent ability to press forward despite overwhelming odds suggests a high level of resilience. He may use determination and a strong will to persevere through emotionally distressing situations.

  C. Escapism and Distraction: Freeman's focus on immediate tasks, such as combatting alien threats, may serve as a distraction from the emotional turmoil caused by the catastrophic events around him. Engaging in action and problem-solving activities might provide him with a temporary reprieve from emotional distress.

  D. Quiet Moments of Reflection: Although not explicitly shown, Freeman's moments of silence and contemplation during quieter times could be interpreted as his way of processing emotions and reflecting on the events he has witnessed.

- Outcomes: The effectiveness of coping strategies can lead to different outcomes. Successful coping may result in reduced stress, improved well-being, and a sense of mastery over the situation. In contrast, ineffective coping may lead to increased stress, emotional distress, and a sense of helplessness.

- Reappraisal: Over time, individuals may continuously reappraise the situation, adjusting their coping strategies based on the evolving circumstances and their perceived effectiveness.

Lazarus's Transactional Model emphasizes that the experience of stress is not solely determined by external events but is heavily influenced by an individual's cognitive appraisal of those events and their coping responses. It highlights the dynamic and subjective nature of stress and coping, recognizing that different individuals may respond differently to the same stressor based on their appraisals and coping resources. This model has been influential in the field of psychology and has contributed to our understanding of how people adapt to and manage stress in various life situations. Freeman has been through a lot. He's processed the events in multiple ways. He used everything he knew, and demonstrated resilience, constant vigilance and adaptivity to navigate the unpredictable challenges in these distressing situations.

BIOSHOCK

In BioShock, Jack finds himself stranded in the underwater city of Rapture after surviving a plane crash. The wealthy and visionary Andrew Ryan built Rapture as a utopian society for artists, scientists, and industry leaders to thrive without government interference. However, the city has since fallen into chaos due to a substance called ADAM, which grants superhuman abilities but also leads to addiction and genetic mutations. Jack navigates through the decaying and hostile environment of Rapture, uncovering its dark history and unraveling the events that led to its downfall. Jack meets Atlas, who serves as his guide and ally in the beginning, aiding him in his quest to survive and escape the city. BioShock revolves around the consequences of unchecked scientific progress, the dangers of extreme ideologies, and the ethical implications of power.

CHALLENGES

Jack faces a series of hardships and challenges as he navigates through the crumbling and dangerous city of Rapture:

- Isolation and Unknown Environment: Jack starts by surviving a plane crashing into the ocean and then finds himself in the underwater city of Rapture. He is isolated from the surface and must navigate an unfamiliar and hostile environment.

- Splicers and Mutated Creatures: Rapture is filled with "Splicers," genetically modified citizens who have become addicted to ADAM and have gone insane. These Splicers are violent and dangerous, and they attack Jack on sight. Additionally, there are mutated creatures like "Big Daddies" and "Little Sisters" that pose significant threats.
- Resource Scarcity: Supplies, including ammunition and health-restoring items, are limited. Jack must scavenge and manage his resources carefully to survive in the harsh conditions of Rapture.
- Morally Complex Decisions: Throughout his journey, Jack encounters "Little Sisters," young girls who harvest ADAM from corpses. He must decide whether to rescue or harvest ADAM from them, leading to different outcomes and moral consequences.
- Power Struggles: As Jack progresses, he learns about the conflict between Andrew Ryan and Dr. Sofia Lamb, two prominent figures in Rapture's history. Their ideologies clash, and Jack gets caught in the middle of their power struggles, affecting his journey and choices.
- Uncovering Dark Truths: Jack gradually uncovers the dark history of Rapture, including its rise and fall, the origin of ADAM, and the questionable experiments conducted by its residents. These revelations challenge his understanding of the world around him.
- Twists and Betrayals: Many unexpected twists and betrayals constantly challenge Jack's perceptions and goals.

Overall, Jack's journey in BioShock is marked by physical challenges, moral dilemmas, and a relentless exploration of the psychological and ethical consequences of the choices he makes in the unforgiving and enigmatic world of Rapture.

PSYCHOLOGY

The hardships that Jack faces in BioShock have a profound impact on his mental state. The combination of isolation, danger, moral dilemmas, and the unraveling of Rapture's dark history all contribute to shaping Jack's mindset throughout his journey:

- Isolation and Unknown Environment: Being thrust into an unfamiliar and isolated underwater city immediately puts Jack under immense psychological stress. The absence of familiar surroundings and the feeling of being trapped can lead to heightened anxiety and a sense of vulnerability.

- Constant Threat of Violence: The constant threat from Splicers and other hostile creatures creates a state of hyper-vigilance in Jack. This prolonged state of alertness can lead to increased stress and even contribute to the development of psychological trauma.
- Moral Dilemmas: The choices Jack must make regarding the Little Sisters have a significant impact on his moral compass. These decisions force him to confront the ethical implications of his actions, potentially leading to feelings of guilt, inner conflict, and questioning his own humanity.
- Limited Resources: The scarcity of resources in Rapture forces Jack to ration his supplies and make difficult decisions about when and how to use them. This scarcity mindset can lead to feelings of desperation, frustration, and a constant need to strategize and prioritize survival.
- Uncovering Dark Truths: As Jack uncovers the unsettling history of Rapture and learns about the unethical experiments conducted by its residents, he might experience feelings of shock, disgust, and a sense of betrayal. This new knowledge challenges his worldview and raises questions about the nature of humanity and society.
- Psychological Manipulation: The realization that Jack is entwined in the larger narrative of Rapture and its power struggles can lead to a sense of manipulation and loss of control over his own destiny. This revelation may trigger feelings of confusion and paranoia.
- Twists and Betrayals: The unexpected twists and betrayals that he encounters can lead to a sense of distrust and cynicism. The constant uncertainty about who to trust can contribute to feelings of emotional instability.
- Loneliness and Isolation: Jack's lack of companionship and genuine human connection in Rapture can lead to feelings of loneliness and emotional detachment. The absence of positive social interactions can further impact his psychological well-being.
- Survival Instincts: The need to constantly prioritize survival and navigate dangerous situations can lead to the development of a

survival-focused mindset. This can influence decision-making and lead to a more pragmatic and utilitarian approach to challenges.

Overall, the accumulation of these hardships and challenges shape Jack's mindset. The combination of physical danger, moral ambiguity, and the uncovering of unsettling truths creates a complex and multifaceted psychological portrait.

THE BIOPSYCHOSOCIAL MODEL & JACK

The Biopsychosocial model is a comprehensive approach to understanding human health and behavior that considers the interactions between biological, psychological, and social factors. This model recognizes that individuals are complex beings influenced by a combination of biological processes, psychological experiences, and social contexts. Here's a brief overview of each component of the model:

- Biological Factors: These encompass genetic predispositions, neurological processes, and physiological functions. Biological factors can influence how individuals respond to stress, process emotions, and interact with their environment. In the context of Jack's analysis, his genetic makeup, brain chemistry, and physiological responses to stressors would be considered.
  - Genetic Predisposition: Jack's genetic makeup might contribute to his ability to handle stress and make decisions. Some people are naturally more resilient, while others might be more prone to anxiety or impulsive behavior.
  - Neurological Processes: Jack's brain chemistry and neural pathways influence his emotional responses and decision-making. Stressors in Rapture could trigger the release of stress hormones, impacting his behavior and cognitive functions.
  - Physiological Responses: The constant threat of danger triggers Jack's fight-or-flight response, leading to heightened alertness and stress. His physiological responses to danger might vary based on his genetic predispositions.
- Psychological Factors: These involve cognitive processes, emotions, personality traits, and mental health. Psychological

factors shape how individuals perceive and interpret their experiences, make decisions, and cope with challenges. Jack's emotional reactions, cognitive appraisals of danger and moral dilemmas, and potential psychological vulnerabilities would fall under this category.

- Personality Traits: Jack's personality traits, such as empathy, courage, and adaptability, influence his reactions to moral dilemmas and challenges in Rapture. These traits affect how he interacts with other characters and navigates the environment.
- Coping Mechanisms: Jack's coping mechanisms, developed through his upbringing and experiences, shape how he deals with stress. His choices regarding the "Little Sisters" can reflect his coping strategies and emotional regulation.
- Emotional Responses: Jack's emotional responses to isolation, danger, and revelations about Rapture's history play a significant role in his decision-making and overall psychological well-being. His emotions could range from fear and anger to curiosity and determination.

- Social Factors: Social factors include the environment in which an individual lives, their social relationships, cultural influences, and societal norms. These factors can shape a person's behavior, social interactions, and identity. In Jack's case, his isolation in Rapture, interactions with other characters like Atlas and Little Sisters, and exposure to the unique social dynamics of the city would be part of the analysis.

- Social Isolation: Being isolated in Rapture affects Jack's social interactions and emotional well-being. The lack of meaningful connections can lead to loneliness, impacting his mental health.
- Interactions with Others: Jack's interactions with others, such as Atlas, Little Sisters, and other survivors, shape his understanding of the city and his role within it. These interactions impact his sense of purpose and moral compass.
- Cultural and Societal Context: Rapture's unique social and cultural context, driven by Andrew Ryan's ideologies, influences Jack's perceptions of morality, power, and

individualism. The distorted values of Rapture's society impact his decisions.

The Biopsychosocial model emphasizes that Jack's responses and behaviors in Rapture result from the intricate interplay between biological, psychological, and social factors. His genetic predispositions influence his brain chemistry and stress responses, which in turn affect his emotional reactions and cognitive appraisals of situations. His personality traits and coping mechanisms influence how he navigates the challenges of Rapture, while his interactions with others and the city's social context further shape his psychological experience. This model highlights that understanding Jack's psychology requires considering the multifaceted aspects of his being, as no single factor can fully explain his actions and decisions. It provides a holistic framework to analyze his journey through Rapture and the complex interrelationships between his biology, psychology, and social environment.

WHAT CAN WE LEARN?

Jack is resilient; he adapts, he reflects on his life and choices and considers the ethical implications of his actions. He is curious and thinks critically. He understands that everyday life isn't black or white and that everything is more complex than it seems. He continues to uncover the truth, even though it might be unsettling. His journey encourages self-reflection and the idea that people can evolve and adapt their values over time. Be like Jack - reflect, adapt and recognize the complexities of human nature and the power of choice.

NIGHT IN THE WOODS

"Night in the Woods" is developed by Infinite Fall and published by Finji. Margaret "Mae" Borowski is a young adult cat who has dropped out of college and returned to her hometown of Possum Springs, a small, declining mining town. Her Grandfather just died, and she deals with various personal issues, including depression and a sense of aimlessness. She tries to make sense of her life, relationships, and the changes happening in her hometown. Her journey explores themes of mental health, identity, friendship, and the struggles of transitioning into adulthood. As she progresses, Mae uncovers a supernatural element involving strange occurrences and dreams and along with her friends, they embark on an adventure to uncover the truth behind these strange events.

CHALLENGES

Mae Borowski faces several challenges and struggles throughout her journey:

- Mental Health Issues: She grapples with depression and anxiety, which are depicted realistically. Her mental health issues affect her relationships with her friends and family.
- Reconnecting with Friends: After dropping out of college, Mae has to reconnect with her childhood friends, including Bea, Gregg,

and Angus. Rebuilding these friendships and dealing with their own issues becomes a central challenge for her.

- Identity and Purpose: Mae struggles with questions of identity and purpose. She's unsure about her place in the world and often feels lost and aimless, a common theme among many young adults.
- Small Town Decline: Possum Springs, Mae's hometown, is facing economic decline, and the town's residents are dealing with job loss and a sense of hopelessness. Mae has to confront the changes in her hometown and the impact on its residents.
- Supernatural Mystery: As she progresses, Mae and her friends become embroiled in a supernatural mystery involving strange occurrences and dreams. They must unravel the mystery and face the eerie and unsettling aspects of their town.
- Personal Relationships: Mae's relationships with her friends and family evolve throughout her journey. Navigating the complexities of these relationships and addressing conflicts and misunderstandings is an ongoing challenge.
- Growing Up and Adulthood: The transition from adolescence to adulthood, a period filled with uncertainty, responsibilities, and difficult choices confront Mae and her friends who must come to terms with growing up and facing the realities of life.
- Personal Demons: Mae must confront her own inner demons and past mistakes, which are tied to the town's history and her own family's secrets.

PSYCHOLOGY

Mae is deeply affected by the hardships and challenges she faces. She undergoes significant changes, and these challenges have a profound impact on her mental and emotional state:

- Depression and Anxiety: Mae's struggles with depression and anxiety are central to her character. These conditions affect her mood, energy levels, and overall outlook on life. They can make her feel isolated, overwhelmed, and disconnected from the world around her.
- Isolation and Loneliness: Her feelings of aimlessness and her decision to drop out of college contribute to her sense of isolation. She often feels disconnected from her friends and

family, leading to a sense of loneliness that adds to her emotional burden.

- Guilt and Regret: Mae carries a sense of guilt and regret related to past events, which are gradually revealed. These feelings weigh heavily on her and impact her self-esteem and overall mental well-being.
- Relationship Struggles: Her relationships with her friends and family are strained at times due to her mental health issues and the challenges they all face. Her inability to communicate her feelings effectively can lead to conflicts and misunderstandings, further affecting her psychological state.
- Existential Crisis: Mae grapples with questions about her identity, purpose, and the meaning of life. Her existential crisis is exacerbated by the decline of her hometown, which adds to her sense of hopelessness and uncertainty about the future.
- Fear and Uncertainty: The supernatural elements around her contribute to her fear and uncertainty. The strange occurrences and unsettling dreams add to her anxiety and feelings of unease.
- Acceptance and Growth: Mae experiences personal growth and development. She gradually comes to terms with her mental health issues, her past mistakes, and her place in the world. This process of acceptance and growth is essential to her psychological well-being.

"Night in the Woods" explores these psychological aspects with a high degree of realism and sensitivity and is a unique opportunity to empathize with Mae's struggles and challenges, shedding light on the complexities of mental health, personal growth, and the human experience.

THE BIOPSYCHOSOCIAL MODEL & MAE

The Biopsychosocial Model is a holistic approach to understanding and explaining human health and well-being. It recognizes that an individual's health and psychological well-being are influenced by a complex interplay of biological, psychological, and social factors. This model was developed as an alternative to the traditional biomedical model, which primarily focuses on biological factors in health and illness. Analyzing Mae using the Biopsychosocial Model can give us valuable insights into the challenges she faces while taking into account the interconnectedness of biological, psychological, and social factors.

- Biological Factors: This aspect of the model considers the physical and genetic aspects of a person's health. It includes factors such as genetics, hormones, neurotransmitters, and the functioning of bodily systems. Biological factors can influence an individual's susceptibility to certain illnesses and their overall physical health. In the context of mental health, imbalances in neurotransmitters like serotonin or genetic predispositions to conditions like depression are examples of biological factors. This aspect considers Mae's biological makeup, including her genetic predispositions and neurochemistry. Her struggles with depression and anxiety may have biological underpinnings, such as imbalances in neurotransmitters like serotonin. The model acknowledges that her mental health challenges are not solely a result of her personality or circumstances.
- Psychological Factors: Psychological factors encompass a person's thoughts, emotions, behaviors, and cognitive processes. These factors play a crucial role in mental health and well-being. Psychological theories and models, such as cognitive-behavioral therapy (CBT), psychodynamic theory, and humanistic psychology, are used to understand how thoughts, emotions, and behaviors contribute to mental health conditions and overall psychological functioning. Mae's psychological factors involve her thoughts, emotions, and behavior. Her depression, anxiety, and feelings of guilt and regret are essential elements to consider.
- Social Factors: Social factors refer to the impact of an individual's social environment and relationships on their health. These factors include family dynamics, social support networks, socioeconomic status, cultural influences, and environmental stressors. Social factors can have a profound influence on a person's mental health and can contribute to conditions such as stress, depression, and anxiety. Mae's environment and social context play a significant role in her psychological well-being. The decline of her hometown, Possum Springs, and the economic challenges faced by its residents contribute to her sense of hopelessness and isolation.

The Biopsychosocial Model acknowledges that these three components are interconnected and influence one another. For example, biological factors (e.g., genetics) can predispose someone to a mental health condition, while psychological factors (e.g., negative thought patterns) and social factors (e.g., a lack of social support) can exacerbate or mitigate the condition's severity. This model is widely used in healthcare, psychology, and psychiatry to provide a more comprehensive understanding of an individual's health and well-being. It emphasizes the importance of considering all three domains when assessing and treating health conditions. By taking a holistic approach, healthcare professionals can develop more effective interventions and treatment plans that address the multifaceted nature of an individual's health and psychological state.

WHAT CAN WE LEARN?

Mae is going through a struggle. Instead of staring at the ceiling (like I did for quite a while) she found little things that could help her get through it and stuck with them. Moving home to be closer to her family and the community, reconnecting with friends, finding a larger purpose to aim towards - all of these help Mae go forward day by day till she gets out of this rough time. Mae is more relatable than others because she goes through struggles that many human beings go through.

HEAVY RAIN

The main character "Heavy Rain", developed by Quantic Dream, is Ethan Mars. His storyline is one of the four interwoven narratives. Mars is a loving father and husband who lives a normal life with his wife Grace and their two sons, Jason and Shaun. However, tragedy strikes when, during a family outing at a mall, Ethan loses his younger son, Jason, in a tragic accident. This event deeply traumatized him and led to the breakdown of his marriage. Ethan desperately searches for his missing son, Shaun, after receiving mysterious letters from a serial killer, "Origami Killer," who abducts young boys and drowns them in rainwater after a period of captivity. These letters contain instructions for a series of trials and challenges that Ethan must complete to prove his love for his son and ultimately save him from the clutches of the killer. Ethan embarks on this harrowing journey, facing numerous moral and physical challenges. His storyline is filled with intense emotional moments and his actions have consequences for both him and others in his journey. Other characters in Heavy rain include a private investigator, an FBI profiler, and a journalist, all of whom are connected in some way to the hunt for the Origami Killer.

CHALLENGES

Ethan Mars faces a series of challenging trials and obstacles set by the Origami Killer. The trials are designed to test Ethan's love and determination in his quest to save his missing son, Shaun.

- The Lizard Trial: The first trial involves Ethan cutting off the last section of one of his own fingers and placing it in a box as a gruesome proof of his commitment. This act of self-mutilation is emotionally and physically distressing for him.
- The Butterfly Trial: In this trial, Ethan must navigate a dangerous and busy highway during a heavy rainstorm. He must walk against traffic, jump over obstacles, and dodge oncoming cars to reach a specific location while trying to avoid getting hit.
- The Shark Trial: For this trial, Ethan must crawl through a narrow, dark tunnel filled with broken glass and sharp objects. The objective is to reach the end of the tunnel to find a clue about Shaun's whereabouts.
- The Bear Trial: In this trial, Ethan is confronted with a violent, aggressive drug dealer. To get information from the dealer, Ethan must fight him and potentially kill him, depending on his choices.
- The Rat Trial: In the final trial, Ethan must complete a series of puzzles and challenges within a time limit to locate and rescue Shaun, who is trapped in a well filled with rainwater. The outcome of this trial has a significant impact on the ending.

These trials are emotionally and psychologically taxing for Ethan, and he must make choices that can have far-reaching consequences. The challenges are designed to push Ethan to his limits and test his devotion to his son.

PSYCHOLOGY

Ethan Mars's journey has a profound impact on his psychology and emotional well-being. These trials put him through extreme physical and psychological stress, and they contribute to his character's complex and multi-dimensional portrayal.

- Emotional Trauma: The trauma of losing his younger son, Jason, in a tragic accident already left Ethan emotionally scarred. The loss of a child is a traumatic event, and it is evident that Ethan is haunted by guilt and grief.
- Desperation and Determination: Ethan's love for his remaining son, Shaun, drives him to take on the Origami Killer's trials despite their horrific nature. His determination to save Shaun is unwavering, and this desperation to reunite with his son compels

him to push through the challenges despite the physical and emotional toll they take.

- Guilt and Self-Loathing: Ethan's self-mutilation in the Lizard Trial is an act of desperation, and it reflects the depths of his guilt and self-loathing. He believes that he deserves to suffer for failing to protect his sons.
- Physical and Mental Strain: The physical trials, such as crawling through the dark, glass-filled tunnel in the Shark Trial or risking his life on a dangerous highway in the Butterfly Trial, take a toll on Ethan's physical health. The stress and fear associated with these challenges can also lead to mental strain.
- Moral Dilemmas: Throughout his journey, Ethan is faced with morally complex decisions, including violent confrontations and choices that may harm others. These decisions can weigh heavily on his conscience, adding to his psychological burden.
- Multiple Outcomes: Ethan's choices can lead to various outcomes. This uncertainty can further affect his mental state, as he is responsible for determining his fate.

Ethan's journey in "Heavy Rain" is marked by his struggle to come to terms with his past, his determination to save his son, and the psychological toll of the trials he endures.

FREUD'S STRUCTURAL MODEL OF THE MIND & ETHAN

Sigmund Freud's "Structural Model of the Mind" consists of three components: the id, the ego, and the superego. These three elements work together to shape an individual's thoughts, behaviors, and motivations. They can be used to analyze Ethan and provide insights into his internal conflicts and motivations:

- The Id: The id is the most primitive and instinctual part of the mind. It operates on the pleasure principle, seeking immediate gratification of basic needs and desires. The id is concerned with fulfilling biological and psychological needs, such as hunger, thirst, and pleasure. It is impulsive, irrational, and operates without regard for reality or consequences. For example, if a person is hungry, the id might compel them to grab and eat food without considering social norms or the impact on others. In Ethan's case, his id is primarily focused on the instinctual desire to protect and save his son, Shaun. His intense love and desperation to reunite with him can be seen as manifestations of his id's need for immediate gratification and relief from the emotional pain caused by Jason's death.

- The Ego: The ego is the conscious and rational part of the mind. It develops as a result of the need to deal with the external world and mediate between the demands of the id and the constraints of reality. The ego operates on the reality principle, seeking to satisfy the id's desires in a way that is realistic and socially acceptable. It engages in problem-solving, decision-making, and planning. If the id desires food, the ego might plan a meal, considering factors like time, place, and social context. Ethan's ego is at the forefront as he navigates the complex and dangerous challenges set by the Origami Killer. He must make rational decisions, solve puzzles, and engage in problem-solving to accomplish his goal of finding Shaun.

- Superego: The superego represents the internalized values, morals, and societal standards. It develops through the influence of parents, teachers, and cultural norms. The superego acts as a moral guide, enforcing ethical and social rules. It strives for perfection and punishes the ego for behaviors that violate moral or social standards. If the id wants to take something that doesn't belong to the person, the superego may generate feelings of guilt and remorse, discouraging the action. In Ethan's case, his superego is influenced by his sense of responsibility as a father and his guilt over Jason's death. His superego compels him to make ethical choices and drives him to seek redemption and forgiveness for his perceived failures as a parent.

In Freud's model, the id, ego, and superego are in constant interaction and can be in conflict with each other. The ego attempts to balance the demands of the id and the superego, navigating the individual through the challenges of the external world while considering internal moral and instinctual pressures. Ethan's character can be analyzed through the conflicts and interactions among these three components of his mind. His id drives him to take extreme risks and make sacrifices for the immediate goal of saving Shaun, while his ego helps him navigate the challenges logically and strategically. Simultaneously, his superego influences his moral decisions and compels him to seek a sense of justice and redemption for his past actions. This Freudian analysis provides a framework for understanding the internal dynamics of Ethan's character as he grapples with his emotional turmoil, ethical dilemmas, and the desperate need to rescue his son.

GOD OF WAR

Kratos' journey in "God of War" is complex and includes many challenges. He is introduced as a skilled and ruthless Spartan warrior who serves the Greek gods. He has many nightmares and is haunted by his past, including the murder of his wife and daughter, which he was tricked into committing by the God of War, Ares. He seeks revenge and embarks on a quest to kill him. Along his journey, he encounters various mythical creatures and gods, gaining their powers and abilities. After becoming the new God of War, Kratos seeks to overthrow the gods of Olympus and take their power for himself. He faces off against powerful adversaries such as Mythical Beasts, Zeus and Athena while also learning more about his tragic past. Later on, Kratos tries to escape his past and protect his son, Atreus. Together, they embark on a journey to scatter the ashes of Kratos's wife (Atreus' mother). Kratos is known for his intense anger and brutality, often solving problems through violence. He struggles with his violent nature and attempts to be a better father. He goes through significant development, showing a more humane side and understanding the consequences of his actions.

CHALLENGES

Kratos has faced numerous hardships and challenges throughout his journey.

- The Murder of His Family: One of the earliest and most significant hardships Kratos experiences is being tricked to murder his wife and daughter by the God of War, Ares, as part of a deal to gain immense power which haunts him forever.
- Serving the Gods: Kratos becomes a servant of the Greek gods, particularly Ares. He is forced to do their bidding and participates in brutal wars and conflicts on their behalf.
- Betrayal by the Gods: He seeks revenge against Ares for his past actions, but he faces betrayal and obstacles from other gods, including Athena and Zeus. They see him as a threat and attempt to stop him.
- Epic Battles: Kratos engages in epic battles against powerful foes, including titans, gods, and mythical creatures. These battles push him to his physical and emotional limits.
- Loss of His Godhood: In his quest for revenge against the gods, he eventually loses his own godhood and powers, leaving him vulnerable and mortal. This loss forces him to rely on his own strength and wit.
- Consequences of His Actions: Kratos's violent and ruthless nature often leads to unintended consequences. His actions result in widespread destruction and suffering, and he must confront the repercussions of his choices.
- The Burden of Parenthood: Kratos is trying to be a better father to his son, Atreus. This presents a new set of challenges as he tries to protect and guide his son while wrestling with his own troubled past.

Kratos's journey is marked by a constant struggle against both external and internal challenges. His development involves coming to terms with his past, seeking redemption, and striving to be a better person and parent while dealing with the legacy of his violent actions.

PSYCHOLOGY

The hardships Kratos faces throughout the "God of War" series have a profound impact on his personality, beliefs, and behavior.

- Rage and Anger: Kratos's character is defined by his intense rage and anger, which stem from the murder of his family and his servitude to the gods. These emotions drive him to seek revenge and often lead him to act impulsively and violently.

- Guilt and Regret: Kratos carries an immense burden of guilt and regret for his past actions, especially the murder of his wife and daughter. This guilt haunts him throughout the series and contributes to his internal turmoil.
- Mistrust and Betrayal: Kratos's experiences with the gods, who often betray or manipulate him, lead to a deep-seated mistrust of divine beings and authority figures. He becomes cynical and reluctant to place his trust in anyone.
- Existential Crisis: As Kratos battles gods and titans, he questions the meaning and purpose of his existence. He grapples with his identity as a mortal who was once a god, and this existential crisis drives much of his self-development.
- Desire for Redemption: Despite his violent nature and past deeds, Kratos seeks redemption and a way to atone for his sins. He is haunted by the hope of finding some form of forgiveness or absolution.
- Protectiveness and Fatherhood: Taking care of his son challenges his traditional persona and forces him to confront his own shortcomings as a parent. He strives to protect Atreus and guide him while fearing that his own violent tendencies may negatively influence his son.
- Adaptation to New Realities: Transitioning from Greek to Norse mythology presents Kratos with the challenge of adapting to a completely different world with its own gods, rules, and creatures. This forces him to reevaluate his beliefs and confront his past actions in a new context.

The hardships Kratos endures have a profound impact on his psychology, leading to a complex character who wrestles with a range of emotions and moral dilemmas. His journey is one of redemption, self-acceptance, and attempting to break free from the cycle of violence and vengeance that has defined much of his life.

FREUD'S PSYCHOANALYTIC MODEL & KRATOS

One of the most famous and referred psychological models is the Psychoanalytic model. It was first laid out in the late 19th century by Sigmund Freud, describing the effect of childhood events on the character of an adult. Analyzing Kratos through the Freudian and Jungian psychoanalytic models provides insights into different aspects of his character, motivations, and behavior. If Kratos were to lay on the Freud's couch, he'd probably analyze him like this:

- Id: The primitive and unconscious part of the psyche that seeks immediate gratification of desires, often without consideration for consequences. Kratos exhibits a pronounced id-driven nature. He is characterized by intense and often impulsive desires for revenge, power, and violence. His brutal actions throughout the series reflect his id's pursuit of immediate gratification and the release of pent-up rage.
- Ego: The conscious part of the psyche that mediates between the id's desires and the superego's moral constraints. It seeks to balance impulses with reality. Kratos's character reflects elements of the ego, particularly in his attempts to navigate the real-world challenges and conflicts he encounters. He is often driven by a need to survive and overcome external obstacles, attempting to find a balance between his violent tendencies and his desire for personal redemption.
- Superego: The moral and ethical component of the psyche that internalizes societal norms and values. It serves as the conscience. While Kratos does possess a moral compass, it's significantly overshadowed by his id-driven desires. His superego, which represents societal norms and values, is relatively weak in his character, as he often acts in defiance of traditional moral boundaries.
- By psychoanalytic theory, there are a few Defense Mechanisms - Psychological strategies used by the ego to protect the individual from anxiety and distress. Defense mechanisms can include denial, projection, displacement, repression and regression. Kratos uses several Defence Mechanisms to cope.
    - Displacement: A common defense mechanism in Kratos's character is displacement, where he redirects his intense emotions and anger towards external targets. His violent acts against gods and mythical creatures serve as outlets for the unresolved rage he harbors.
    - Repression: Kratos attempts to repress the traumatic memories of the murder of his family and his own violent actions. These repressed memories resurface in the form of recurring nightmares, symbolizing the unconscious turmoil within him.

- Psychosexual Stages: Freud proposed that human development occurs in distinct stages, each characterized by a focus on different erogenous zones and associated with specific conflicts (e.g., the oral, anal, and genital stages). We won't go into this regarding Kratos, but it is a big part of Freud's theory.
- Unconscious Mind: Freud believed that much of human behavior is influenced by unconscious thoughts, desires, and memories. Much of Kratos's character and actions can be attributed to his unconscious mind, where repressed desires, unresolved conflicts, and traumatic memories influence his behavior. His violent actions are driven by elements of his unconscious, and he experiences nightmares that are manifestations of his unresolved past.

A Freudian psychoanalytic analysis of Kratos reveals a character deeply influenced by his id-driven desires, the use of defense mechanisms to cope with his traumatic past, and the presence of repressed memories and emotions. His character is marked by ongoing internal conflicts and a continual struggle to reconcile his violent tendencies with his pursuit of redemption.

WHAT CAN WE LEARN FROM KRATOS?

Kratos hit rock bottom, lost his family and decided to pursue a higher purpose that keeps him going. Throughout his journey, Kratos experiences emotional growth and introspection. He learns to control his rage and seeks alternative solutions to problems. His journey becomes one of self-discovery and personal transformation.

SILENT HILL 2

James Sunderland, who is featured in Silent Hill 2, is considered one of the most critically acclaimed entries in the series. The adventure begins when James receives a letter from his deceased wife, Mary, asking him to meet her in their "special place" in the mysterious and eerie town of Silent Hill. The letter baffles James because Mary had been dead for three years due to a terminal illness. Driven by a mixture of hope and confusion, James arrives in Silent Hill and quickly finds that the town is engulfed in dense fog and is inhabited by grotesque and nightmarish creatures. As he explores the town, he encounters several other individuals, including Angela Orosco, Eddie Dombrowski, and Laura, a young girl who claims to be looking for her mother. James's journey through Silent Hill is deeply psychological and emotionally charged. He grapples with his own guilt and personal demons related to his wife's illness, which leads to a haunting and introspective exploration of his psyche. The town of Silent Hill itself is often portrayed as a reflection of the characters' inner turmoil, making the atmosphere both unsettling and thought-provoking. Throughout his journey, James must confront not only the terrifying monsters that inhabit Silent Hill but also the dark secrets of his past and the truth behind his wife's letter.

CHALLENGES

James faces a multitude of challenges throughout his nightmarish journey in the town of Silent Hill. These challenges are not only physical but also deeply psychological and emotional.

- Monstrous Threats: Silent Hill is infested with grotesque and disturbing creatures, including Pyramid Head, Nurses, and various other monstrous entities. James must confront and often fight these creatures to survive and progress.
- Puzzles and Obstacles: The town itself is a labyrinth filled with intricate puzzles and obstacles that James must solve to advance. These puzzles are often symbolic and add to the overall atmosphere of mystery and psychological horror.
- Exploring His Own Guilt: One of the central challenges James faces is his own guilt and emotional turmoil related to his wife's illness and death. Silent Hill serves as a manifestation of his inner demons, forcing him to confront his past and come to terms with his actions.
- Interactions with Other Characters: James encounters other characters in Silent Hill, each dealing with their own traumas and issues. Interacting with these characters and understanding their stories is a challenge, as their narratives are intertwined with James's and contribute to the overall mystery.
- Maintaining His Sanity: The town of Silent Hill is known for its ability to warp reality and play tricks on the minds of those who enter. James must grapple with hallucinations, disturbing imagery, and an ever-shifting environment, all of which challenge his sanity.
- Emotional Catharsis: Ultimately, the most significant challenge for James is achieving emotional catharsis and closure regarding his wife's death and his own role in it. This requires him to delve deep into his psych and make choices that lead to different emotional resolutions.

PSYCHOLOGY

The challenges that James Sunderland faces in Silent Hill 2 have a profound impact on his psychology and mental state throughout his journey. The atmosphere is designed to explore the depths of his psyche, and the challenges he encounters serve to exacerbate his emotional and psychological struggles. James' mind is filled with:

- Guilt and Self-Reflection: His primary psychological challenge is dealing with overwhelming guilt and self-doubt related to his wife Mary's illness and death. The town of Silent Hill reflects his inner turmoil, making him confront his actions and decisions. This constant self-reflection leads to a heightened sense of guilt and self-loathing.
- Hallucinations and Disturbing Imagery: As James explores Silent Hill, he encounters disturbing hallucinations and nightmarish imagery. These visual and auditory distortions warp his perception of reality, contributing to his growing sense of disorientation and mental instability.
- Emotional Turmoil: James' emotional state is continuously tested. His encounters with other characters dealing with their traumas, as well as the unraveling mystery of the town, further exacerbate his emotional turmoil. James knows that his actions can lead to different emotional outcomes - affecting his mental well-being.
- Isolation and Loneliness: Silent Hill is a desolate and isolated town, amplifying James's feelings of loneliness and isolation. The absence of other human beings, except for the occasional eerie encounters with other characters, adds to his sense of being trapped in his own mind.
- Fear and Anxiety: The constant threat of grotesque monsters and the unpredictable nature of Silent Hill's environment instill fear and anxiety in James. These emotions further erode his mental stability, making it challenging for him to distinguish between reality and hallucination.
- Desperation and Obsession: James's determination to uncover the truth behind his wife's letter drives him to obsessive behavior. His desperate quest for closure and answers fuels his psychological descent, as he becomes more and more entangled in the mysteries of Silent Hill.

The challenges James faces are intricately tied to his psychological journey. His journey explores themes of guilt, grief, trauma, and self-discovery that delve into the darkest corners of the human psyche.

JUNG'S PSYCHOANALYTIC MODEL & JAMES

The Jungian psychoanalytic model, developed by Swiss psychiatrist Carl Gustav Jung, is a psychological framework that focuses on the exploration of the unconscious mind, individuation, archetypes, and the collective unconscious. It offers a unique perspective on human psychology and is often contrasted with Sigmund Freud's psychoanalysis. Here's how some key aspects of the model can be applied to understanding James:

- Collective Unconscious: Jung proposed the existence of a "collective unconscious," which is a part of the unconscious mind shared by all humans. It contains universal experiences, symbols, and archetypes that shape human behavior and thought. This collective unconscious is distinct from an individual's personal unconscious, which houses their unique experiences and memories. The town of Silent Hill serves as a symbolic representation of the collective unconscious. It is a place where deep, universal human fears, traumas, and archetypal elements manifest.

- Archetypes: Archetypes are universal symbols, themes, and patterns that appear in myths, folklore, dreams, and human culture across different times and places. Jung believed that these archetypes are innate and influence human thought and behavior. Examples of archetypes include the Hero, the Shadow, the Anima/Animus, and the Wise Old Man. The monsters, disturbing imagery, and psychological horrors encountered by James can be seen as archetypal representations of his inner conflicts and fears. For example, Pyramid Head may symbolize aspects of the Shadow archetype, representing James's own hidden and darker tendencies. We'll go deeper into archetypes in the next chapter.

- Individuation: Jung's concept of individuation refers to the process of becoming one's true and unique self. It involves integrating aspects of the unconscious, resolving inner conflicts, and achieving a sense of wholeness. Individuation is a central goal of Jungian psychoanalysis and is often seen as a path to self-realization. James's journey through Silent Hill can be viewed as a quest for individuation and self-realization. He is confronted with repressed emotions, guilt, and the need to integrate his own

Shadow – the darker aspects of his personality, which is a key component of the individuation process in Jungian psychology.

- Personality Types: Jung introduced the idea of personality types based on cognitive functions. His theory laid the groundwork for the development of the Myers-Briggs Type Indicator (MBTI), which categorizes individuals into 16 personality types based on preferences for functions like introversion or extraversion and thinking or feeling. We'll get to this model in a later chapter (hint: Lara Croft).

- The Self: The Self is a central concept in Jungian psychology. It represents the totality of an individual's psyche, including both the conscious and unconscious aspects. Achieving self-realization is seen as the ultimate goal of psychological development. James begins his journey fragmented, with repressed guilt, unresolved emotions, and a distorted perception of reality. His journey through Silent Hill is, in part, a quest for integration and a confrontation with the various aspects of his own psyche.

- Dream Analysis: Jung placed significant emphasis on dream analysis. He believed that dreams provide a window into the unconscious mind and can reveal insights into an individual's inner conflicts, unresolved issues, and the archetypal elements at play in their psyche. James's entire journey can be seen as a surreal, dream-like experience where he confronts his inner demons and repressed emotions. The symbolism and bizarre occurrences mirror the symbolic nature of dreams, providing insight into James's psyche.

- Integration of the Shadow: The "Shadow" is a key concept in Jungian psychology, representing the darker, hidden aspects of an individual's personality. Jung believed that embracing and integrating the Shadow is essential for personal growth and individuation. A central theme in Silent Hill is James's confrontation with his own Shadow, which is reflected in the town's monstrous inhabitants and his journey to understand his repressed guilt and emotions. Jungian psychology suggests that embracing and integrating the Shadow is a vital step toward individuation and achieving a sense of wholeness. James's willingness to confront his own dark side and accept responsibility for his actions is a central aspect of his character development.

The Jungian psychoanalytic model is known for its emphasis on the deeper layers of the human psyche, the exploration of archetypal symbolism, and the pursuit of personal growth and self-realization. It has had a significant influence not only in psychology but also in fields like literature, art, and mythology. Overall, applying the Jungian psychoanalytic model to James Sunderland's character highlights the deep exploration of the unconscious, the role of archetypes and symbolism, and the journey toward individuation and self-realization. It underscores the psychological complexity and its use of psychological horror as a means to delve into the depths of the human psyche.

DANGEROUS DAVE

In "Dangerous Dave", developed by John Romero, Dave, a brave but not-so-smart character, is on a quest to save his little brother Delbert from the evil Dr. Nemesis. Dave is depicted as an ordinary guy with no extraordinary abilities, but he possesses strong determination. Despite his lack of special powers, he ventures into dangerous environments, facing various hazards and enemies, relying solely on his wits and platforming skills to survive. Some of the common obstacles he encounters include spikes, pits, lava, moving platforms, and enemy creatures. The goal is to reach the end of each level while collecting as many treasures as possible and avoiding deadly traps. Dave only has one life, and if he loses it, he has to start his journey from the beginning.

CHALLENGES

Dave has many challenges he has to deal with throughout his journey:
- Platforming Challenges: Dave must jump and maneuver precisely so as not to fall into any gaps. Hope he's done his squats.
- Deadly Traps: If he does fall into one of the gaps, it could often be into spikes, fire, water and some form of weird algae. He must time himself carefully.
- Hostile Creatures: Dave encounters various hostile creatures and enemies that can harm him. These enemies might move in

patterns, requiring him to strategize and find the best way to defeat or bypass them.

- Puzzles: Sometimes Dave has to manipulate objects and interact with them in order to move on.
- Timed Sections: If it wasn't scary till now, in certain areas, he faces timed challenges where he must move quickly to avoid being crushed or caught by hazards that move on a set schedule.
- Limited Lives: One of the fundamental challenges is the limited number of chances Dave has. If Dave loses all his lives, he has to restart his journey from the beginning.
- Limited Resources: He must save up the limited ammunition he has for his gun, adding a resource management aspect.
- Boss Battles: Dave sometimes has to face evil bosses - and to beat them he needs precise timing and a sound strategy.
- Orientation: Sometimes he can get lost or disoriented navigating throughout the maze-like world.

PSYCHOLOGY

So, we know that Dave is simple and relatable - embodying a classic hero on a quest to save his brother. The turmoil he has been through has shaped the way he thinks and behaves.

- Determination and bravery: Dave's unwavering determination to save his brother from danger showcases bravery and a strong sense of responsibility.
- Risk-taking and impulsivity: Dave has a fearless approach to danger and his willingness to take risks without much consideration for consequences.
- Problem-Solving and Adaptability: To reach his brother, Dave must quickly adapt to different obstacles and find solutions to various problems.
- Goal-oriented behavior: Dave's single-minded focus on rescuing his brother demonstrates goal-oriented behavior.

JUNG'S THEORY OF ARCHETYPES & DAVE

A psychological model that could be used to analyze Dave's is Carl Jung's theory of archetypes. This model can help us understand the underlying symbolic and psychological aspects of Dave's character. Jung was originally a follower of Sigmund Freud but disagreed when Freud put an emphasis on sexuality during development. This led Jung to develop his own approach known as analytical psychology. He agreed that the unconscious plays an important part in a human's development but expanded to include the collective unconscious. This suggests that archetypes are universal, recurring symbols and themes that exist within the collective unconscious of all humans and history is full of them. These archetypes represent fundamental human experiences, values, personalities and motivations. We can use Jung's theory to explore the deeper symbolic meanings and motivations behind Dave's behavior. This model provides a way to interpret his character beyond his immediate actions and challenges, delving into the universal themes and psychological underpinnings that drive his journey.

There are a few important points about Jung's theory to consider before analyzing Dave. First, Jung's theory suggests that there is a collective unconscious shared with everyone which has a shared repository of human experiences and images. The different archetypes arise from it. They are characteristics and traits that form symbolic patterns that are thought to be universal and deeply ingrained in human psychology. They represent fundamental aspects of the human experience that transcend cultural and individual differences. These archetypes are seen in myths, folklore and different story mediums. While there were four major archetypes (Persona, Shadow, Anima/Animus, Self) there is no limit to how many can exist. They have Psychological Depth, underlying motivations and symbolic meanings. Each character can embody multiple archetypes simultaneously or shift through them as the story unfolds.

So, what kind of Archetype is Dave? Well, obviously a Hero. But he also has a bit of other Archetypes in him that influence his behavior and interactions.

- The Hero: The Hero archetype represents a character who embarks on a journey or quest, often facing challenges and overcoming obstacles to achieve a goal. Dave's role as the protagonist in "Dangerous Dave," rescuing his brother from danger, aligns with the Hero archetype. His determination, bravery, and willingness to confront dangers make him a classic example of this archetype.
- The Everyman: The Everyman archetype represents relatable, ordinary individuals who are placed in extraordinary circumstances. Dave's character is also the Everyman archetype,

as he is a regular person faced with the extraordinary task of rescuing his brother. This archetype can evoke a sense of empathy from others who can relate to his situation.

- The Caregiver: The Caregiver archetype is concerned with nurturing, protecting, and selflessly caring for others. Dave's motivation to rescue his brother reflects the Caregiver archetype, as he is driven by the desire to protect and provide for his sibling's safety.
- The Explorer: The Explorer archetype represents individuals who are curious, adventurous, and eager to explore new territories and experiences. Dave's willingness to venture into dangerous environments and face unknown challenges aligns with the Explorer archetype.
- The Jester: The Jester archetype embodies playfulness, humor, and a tendency to defy conventions. While this archetype might not be as strong in Dave's character, his sometimes-reckless behavior and the whimsical nature of the challenges could evoke elements of the Jester archetype.

So, what can we learn from Dave? Perseverance in the face of adversity? Not giving up easily (or at all)? Does he encourage you to embrace a more adventurous mindset? Critical Thinking? Problem solving skills? Can you, like him, set clear objectives and work hard to achieve them? Can you learn from your failures and persevere? Can you keep on improving your skills through repetition and practice? And what can we learn from Jung, having his model not being viewed favorably in modern psychology....The same maybe?

TOMB RAIDER

Lara Croft is an archaeologist and adventurer known for her intelligence, physical prowess, and resourcefulness. Lara becomes stranded on a mysterious island in the Dragon's Triangle after her ship crashes during a violent storm. She must learn to survive in this hostile environment, confront dangerous enemies, and uncover the island's dark secrets. She transforms from a vulnerable young woman to a skilled and determined explorer. She faces ancient mysteries, uncovers lost civilizations and battles various adversaries. Lara Croft is a complex and multifaceted character, driven by her passion for archaeology and a desire to uncover the truth, often at great personal risk. Her intelligence, resourcefulness, and determination are key attributes that help her overcome the challenges she faces in her quest for discovery and adventure.

CHALLENGES

Throughout her journeys, Lara Croft faces a wide range of challenges and obstacles as she embarks on her adventures.

- Environmental Hazards: She often finds herself in hostile and treacherous environments. She must navigate through dense jungles, icy mountain peaks, underground caves, and ancient tombs.
- Puzzles and Riddles: Lara must solve intricate puzzles and riddles to progress. These puzzles often involve deciphering ancient

inscriptions, manipulating objects, and understanding the mechanics of complex contraptions.

- Combat: Lara encounters various enemies, including mercenaries, cultists, and supernatural creatures. She needs to engage in combat using firearms, melee attacks, and stealth to defeat these adversaries and survive.
- Platforming and Parkour: A significant portion of her journey involves moving across platforms using parkour. She needs to jump, climb, swing, and run across precarious ledges, collapsing structures, and other obstacles.
- Resource Management: Lara must scavenge for resources like food, ammunition, and materials to craft weapons and gear. Managing these resources is crucial for staying alive and progressing.
- Boss Battles: At various points, She encounters powerful adversaries or supernatural beings that require strategic thinking and combat skills to defeat.
- Exploration: Lara is encouraged to explore every nook and cranny of the world to discover hidden tombs, relics, and secrets that provide valuable rewards and insights.

PSYCHOLOGY

Throughout her journey, Lara Croft faces numerous hardships and challenges that have a significant impact on her psychology and character. These hardships shape her into a strong and resilient individual but also take a toll on her mental and emotional well-being.

- Desensitization to Violence: Lara begins her journey as a relatively inexperienced and compassionate archaeologist. As she faces dangerous enemies and life-threatening situations, she becomes desensitized to violence. Killing becomes a necessary means of survival, and this transformation weighs on her conscience. She often struggles with the moral implications of her actions.
- Survival Instincts and Resourcefulness: Lara's hardships force her to develop survival instincts and resourcefulness. She learns to adapt quickly to new environments, assess threats, and make split-second decisions. This heightened awareness and ability to adapt become crucial to her survival.

- **Resilience:** Lara's resilience is tested repeatedly as she faces seemingly insurmountable odds. Her ability to endure physical and emotional pain, push through challenges, and persevere in the face of adversity becomes a defining trait. Her determination to uncover the truth and complete her quests helps her overcome the most daunting challenges.
- **Emotional Struggles:** Lara's journey is fraught with emotional struggles. She grapples with feelings of guilt and responsibility for the fates of those around her. The loss of friends and allies throughout her adventures takes a heavy toll on her emotional well-being, and she must find ways to cope with grief and trauma.
- **Isolation:** Many times, Lara finds herself isolated in remote and dangerous locations. The isolation can lead to feelings of loneliness and desperation, further impacting her mental state. It also intensifies her sense of self-reliance.
- **Determination and Obsession:** Lara's unwavering determination to uncover the truth and solve ancient mysteries can border on obsession. Her relentless pursuit of answers can sometimes cloud her judgment and put her in even greater danger.
- **Strained Relationships:** Lara's adventures sometimes strain her relationships with others, as her quest for knowledge and adventure often takes precedence. She must grapple with the impact of her choices on her relationships with friends and allies.
- **Post-Traumatic Stress:** Given the constant danger and violence she encounters, Lara likely experiences symptoms of post-traumatic stress disorder (PTSD) or other forms of trauma. Flashbacks, nightmares, and emotional triggers may be part of her psychological struggles.

In summary, Lara Croft's psychology is deeply affected by the hardships and challenges she faces. Her development is characterized by a transformation from a young and idealistic archaeologist into a battle-hardened survivor, and her mental and emotional responses to these challenges are integral.

THE MYERS-BRIGGS TYPE INDICATOR & LARA

The Myers-Briggs Type Indicator (MBTI) is a widely used personality assessment tool designed to categorize individuals into one of 16 distinct personality types based on their preferences in four dichotomies. It was developed by Katharine Cook Briggs and her daughter Isabel Briggs Myers, drawing inspiration from Carl Jung's theories of personality. Here are the four dichotomies used in the MBTI:

- Extraversion (E) vs. Introversion (I):
    - Extraversion (E): People who prefer extraversion tend to focus on the external world, are outgoing, and gain energy from interacting with others.
    - Introversion (I): Individuals who prefer introversion focus on their internal world, are reserved, and recharge by spending time alone.
    - Analysis: Lara exhibits traits of both extraversion and introversion. While she can be assertive and action-oriented in her pursuit of treasure, she also values solitude and introspection during her explorations and decision-making processes.
- Sensing (S) vs. Intuition (N):
    - Sensing (S): Those who prefer sensing are practical, detail-oriented, and rely on concrete information obtained through their senses.
    - Intuition (N): Individuals who prefer intuition are imaginative, future-oriented, and focus on patterns and possibilities beyond the immediate sensory data.
    - Lara demonstrates sense and intuition. She relies on her keen senses and practical skills during her expeditions (sensing), but she also relies on intuition to decipher ancient puzzles, uncover hidden meanings, and make connections that go beyond the observable.
- Thinking (T) vs. Feeling (F):
    - Thinking (T): Those who prefer thinking make decisions based on logic and objective analysis, often valuing fairness and consistency.
    - Feeling (F): Individuals who prefer feeling make decisions based on personal values, considering the impact on people and special circumstances.

- Lara often exhibits a thinking-oriented approach, making logical and strategic decisions, especially in the face of danger. However, her character also shows moments of emotional depth and compassion, reflecting a balance between thinking and feeling.
- Judging (J) vs. Perceiving (P):
    - Judging (J): Those who prefer judging prefer structure, organization, and planning. They like to have things settled and decided.
    - Perceiving (P): Individuals who prefer perceiving are flexible, adaptable, and prefer spontaneity. They enjoy keeping their options open.
    - Lara displays a mix of judging and perceiving traits. While she is focused and determined in achieving her goals (judging), she is also adaptable and flexible when facing unexpected challenges (perceiving), adjusting her strategies based on the situation.

When individuals take the MBTI assessment, they are assigned a four-letter code representing their preferences in each dichotomy. For example, an individual might be classified as an ISTJ (Introverted, Sensing, Thinking, Judging) or an ENFP (Extraverted, Intuitive, Feeling, Perceiving). It's essential to note that the MBTI is a tool for understanding preferences rather than fixed traits, and individuals may exhibit a range of behaviors outside their preferred type. With these preferences in mind, Lara's MBTI type could be described as an ISTP (Introverted, Sensing, Thinking, Perceiving) or even an INTJ (Introverted, Intuitive, Thinking, Judging). Both types highlight her independence, practicality, strategic thinking, and adaptability traits that are well-suited to her adventurous and problem-solving lifestyle. Analyzing Lara through Jung's theory provides a framework for understanding her cognitive preferences, decision-making processes, and how she engages with the world around her, adding another layer to the exploration of her character in the Tomb Raider series.

KEEN

In Commander Keen, by id Software, we meet a young 8-year-old boy genius named Billy Blaze, who also goes by the alter ego "Commander Keen." He's a brilliant inventor and a member of the Galaxy Defense Forces, an organization that protects the galaxy from various threats. Billy builds a spaceship in his backyard and sets out on adventures to save the Earth from various alien threats by collecting items and defeating enemies with a pogo stick and raygun.

CHALLENGES

Throughout his journey, Commander Keen faces various challenges and obstacles as he embarks on his intergalactic adventures.

- Alien Enemies: These include the Vorticons, the Shikadi, the Bloogs, the Dopefish, and many others, each with unique abilities and attack patterns. Keen must use his raygun and wits to overcome these foes.
- Platforming: Keen often has to navigate through complex areas filled with obstacles, platforms, and hazards. He must carefully time jumps and movements to avoid falling into pits or getting crushed.
- Collecting Items: Keen needs to collect items such as keycards, ammo, and various power-ups to move on with his journey.

- Limited Resources: Keen's raygun has limited ammunition, so he must manage his shots carefully. Running out of ammo can be challenging, as Keen can't defend himself effectively.
- Battles: Keen must use his wits and reflexes to defeat powerful foes. These battles often require pattern recognition and strategic thinking.
- Gravity Variations: Sometimes, the laws of gravity can be altered, making it challenging to move and jump in unusual ways. Keen needs to adapt to these gravity shifts to progress.
- Environmental Hazards: Keen faces various environmental hazards, such as spikes, lava, water, and electricity. These hazards can quickly end his journey if he's not careful.

Keen needs a combination of quick reflexes, problem-solving skills, and perseverance to overcome the obstacles and adversaries.

PSYCHOLOGY

Keen has been affected by everything that has happened in many ways.

- Resilience: Despite his young age, he takes on various alien adversaries and navigates dangerous environments with determination. This resilience may be seen as a positive psychological trait that allows him to persevere in the face of adversity.
- Problem-Solving Skills: Keen's adventures often require him to solve puzzles, navigate complex levels, and outsmart enemies. These challenges can enhance his problem-solving skills and adaptability.
- Confidence: Successfully overcoming numerous obstacles can boost Keen's confidence. As he progresses through, he becomes more self-assured and capable.
- Courage: Facing alien foes and venturing into unknown territory demonstrates his bravery. This can lead to an increased sense of courage and a willingness to confront difficult situations head-on.
- Independence: We often see him acting independently, relying on his own wit and resourcefulness. This independence may contribute to his self-reliance and ability to make decisions under pressure.

- Stress Management: His ability to handle challenging situations without showing signs of overwhelming stress or anxiety suggests a certain level of emotional resilience.

Overall, Commander Keen is a character who embodies determination and a can-do attitude, making him a beloved figure.

THE FIVE-FACTOR MODEL & KEEN

The Five-Factor Model, also known as the Big Five Personality Traits, is a widely accepted and influential model in the field of personality psychology. It seeks to describe and categorize human personality by identifying five major dimensions of personality traits. These traits are considered to be the fundamental building blocks of individual differences in personality. The five factors are often remembered using the acronym "OCEAN" to represent each dimension:

- Openness to Experience: This factor reflects an individual's openness to new experiences, ideas, and intellectual curiosity. People high in openness tend to be imaginative, creative, and open to trying new things, while those low in openness may be more conventional and resistant to change. Commander Keen exhibits a high level of openness to experience. His curiosity and adventurous nature lead him to explore alien worlds, uncover new challenges, and embrace imaginative and creative solutions to problems.
- Conscientiousness: Conscientiousness relates to an individual's level of organization, responsibility, and self-discipline. People high in conscientiousness are typically organized, dependable, and goal-oriented. Those low in conscientiousness may be more impulsive and less structured in their approach to life. While Commander Keen is a determined and persistent character, his level of conscientiousness may vary depending on the situation. He shows strong organization and responsibility in his missions, carefully navigating complex areas and confronting enemies. However, he may sometimes exhibit impulsive behavior.
- Extraversion: Extraversion pertains to an individual's sociability, assertiveness, and energy levels in social interactions. High extraversion describes outgoing, talkative, and energetic individuals who enjoy socializing, while low extraversion characterizes introverted and reserved individuals who may

prefer solitude or smaller social gatherings. Commander Keen demonstrates a mix of introverted and extraverted traits. He often operates alone on his missions, relying on his own abilities and independence, which reflects introverted tendencies. However, his outgoing and assertive interactions with friendly characters suggest that he has extraverted traits as well.

- Agreeableness: This factor reflects an individual's degree of kindness, cooperation, and consideration of others. High agreeableness indicates people who are compassionate, empathetic, and cooperative, while low agreeableness may describe those who are more competitive or less concerned with the feelings of others. Commander Keen displays agreeableness in his interactions with friendly characters. He helps those in need, showing compassion and empathy. His cooperative nature is evident as he strives to protect Earth from alien threats. However, when facing enemies, he can become more assertive and competitive, which may reflect lower agreeableness in those situations.

- Neuroticism (Emotional Stability): Neuroticism represents an individual's emotional stability and reaction to stress and negative emotions. High neuroticism includes traits such as anxiety, moodiness, and emotional volatility, while low neuroticism describes individuals who are emotionally stable, resilient, and less prone to anxiety and mood swings. Commander Keen demonstrates emotional stability. Despite facing numerous challenges and adversities, he remains calm under pressure and copes with setbacks effectively. He doesn't exhibit high levels of anxiety, moodiness, or emotional volatility, showcasing emotional resilience.

The Five-Factor Model is often assessed using personality inventories, questionnaires, or self-report measures. Respondents answer questions related to each factor, and their responses are used to determine their standing on each trait. This model is a descriptive model, meaning it aims to categorize and describe personality traits rather than explain their underlying causes. These traits are considered relatively stable over time and relatively consistent across different situations and provide a framework for understanding and comparing individual differences in personality. This model is used in fields like psychology, organizational behavior, and counseling and allows for a nuanced understanding of personality by considering the interaction of multiple traits rather than categorizing individuals into rigid personality types. As we can see, Keen is in different areas in each of these different traits.

WHAT CAN WE LEARN?

So, Keen is cool in the face of adventure. When he finds out that planet Earth is under attack, he chooses to go out and save it. He doesn't shy from disgusting slugs, aliens and the different battles he has to go through. He has a higher purpose and decides to do what is right and best for the world.

SONIC THE HEDGEHOG

Sonic the Hedgehog is created by Sega, and the main character is, unsurprisingly, Sonic the Hedgehog himself. He's a blue anthropomorphic hedgehog known for his incredible speed and his trademark red shoes. He is a hero who often finds himself in the role of saving the world from the evil plans of his arch-nemesis, Dr. Robotnik, also known as Dr. Eggman. He is typically portrayed as confident, brave, and a bit cocky. He's known for his love of adventure and his strong sense of justice. He goes on many different adventures that usually revolve around his efforts to thwart Dr. Robotnik's schemes to conquer the world or obtain powerful artifacts. He is sometimes joined by a group of friends known as the "Freedom Fighters" or "Team Sonic," which includes characters like Tails, Knuckles, Amy, and more, each with their unique abilities.

CHALLENGES

Sonic the Hedgehog has faced a wide range of challenges and adversaries throughout his many adventures:

- Dr. Robotnik (Dr. Eggman): Sonic's primary antagonist is the brilliant yet evil scientist, Dr. Robotnik. Robotnik is constantly coming up with new plans to take over the world, and Sonic must thwart his various schemes. These plans often involve capturing animals, turning them into robots (Badniks), and building robotic minions.

- Collecting Chaos Emeralds: One recurring challenge for Sonic is the quest to collect the Chaos Emeralds. These powerful gemstones play a central role as they have the ability to alter reality or grant incredible power. Sonic and his friends often need to gather the Chaos Emeralds before Dr. Robotnik does, to prevent him from achieving his nefarious goals.
- Speed-based platforming: Sonic is known for his incredible speed, and many of his challenges involve high-speed platforming through loop-de-loops, corkscrews, and various obstacles. Players must use Sonic's speed and agility to navigate these levels while avoiding hazards.
- Environmental Hazards: Sonic encounters a variety of environmental hazards, such as bottomless pits, spikes, crushing objects, and underwater sections. These obstacles test his reflexes and platforming skills.
- Boss battles: Sometimes Sonic needs to battle Dr. Robotnik or other formidable foes. These battles often require a combination of strategy and timing to defeat the enemy.
- Time limits: Sometimes Sonic needs to take time limitation into account, adding an element of urgency and pressure.
- Collecting rings: Rings are a staple for Sonic. They serve as both a form of protection (Sonic loses rings instead of a life when hit by an enemy) and a means to gain extra lives or access special areas. Collecting and preserving rings can be crucial to success.
- Teamwork with friends: Many times, Sonic teams up with his friends, each with their unique abilities. He must make sure each of them uses their skillset at the right time in order to complete the mission.

PSYCHOLOGY

Sonic the Hedgehog has a high mental resilience and has a few key traits that show off his psychology. He is primarily a lighthearted and optimistic character, and while he faces numerous challenges and hardships throughout his adventures, these experiences generally do not have a profound negative impact on his psychology.

- Confidence: Sonic is known for his unwavering self-confidence. His ability to face danger head-on, often with a cocky attitude, reflects his belief in his own abilities. Sonic's confidence remains largely unshaken, even in the face of daunting challenges. While this works for Sonic, you can see this trait sometimes as a defense mechanism.
- Determination: Sonic is incredibly determined when it comes to stopping Dr. Robotnik's plans and saving the world. He maintains a strong sense of purpose and refuses to give up, no matter how dire the situation may appear.
- Optimism: Sonic's upbeat and optimistic outlook is a defining trait. He rarely dwells on negativity and instead maintains a positive attitude, believing that he can overcome any obstacle. This optimism helps him stay focused and motivated.
- Resilience: Sonic's ability to bounce back from adversity is a testament to his resilience. Even when he faces setbacks or defeats, he quickly regroups and continues his mission to protect his world.
- Loyalty to Friends: Sonic values his friendships with characters like Tails, Knuckles, and Amy. These relationships provide emotional support and encouragement during challenging times. Sonic's loyalty to his friends strengthens his resolve to overcome obstacles.
- Adaptability: Sonic is known for his adaptability and ability to think on his feet. He often encounters unexpected situations and adapts his strategies accordingly, showcasing his quick thinking and resourcefulness.
- Sense of Justice: Sonic's strong sense of justice drives him to take action against evil and injustice. This moral compass keeps him motivated and focused on his mission.

THE EYSENCK THEORY OF PERSONALITY & SONIC

The Eysenck Personality Questionnaire (EPQ) is a widely used personality assessment tool created by the British psychologist Hans J. Eysenck. The EPQ is designed to measure individual differences in personality traits and is based on Eysenck's theory of personality, which emphasizes two primary dimensions: extraversion / introversion and emotional stability / neuroticism. Later versions of the questionnaire, such as the Revised

Eysenck Personality Questionnaire (EPQ-R), expanded on this theory and added additional dimensions.

- Extraversion (E) vs. Introversion (N): This dimension assesses the extent to which an individual is outgoing, sociable, and enthusiastic (extraversion) or reserved, introspective, and quiet (introversion). High scores on the extraversion scale indicate a more outgoing personality, while low scores suggest introverted tendencies. Sonic demonstrates a high level of extraversion. He is outgoing, adventurous, and enjoys the thrill of high-speed action. Sonic frequently seeks excitement and social interaction, and he's often seen interacting with friends and allies in his adventures. His extroverted nature aligns with the extraversion dimension. So, on this, he gets an E.
- Emotional Stability (S) vs. Neuroticism (N): This dimension measures emotional stability, with individuals scoring high on emotional stability being calm, composed, and emotionally resilient (stability), while those scoring low are more prone to anxiety, moodiness, and emotional reactivity (neuroticism). Sonic exhibits emotional stability. He is typically confident, optimistic, and resilient, even in high-pressure situations. Sonic's ability to stay calm under pressure and maintain a positive attitude aligns with the emotional stability dimension. Give an S to Sonic.
- Psychoticism (P): The third dimension, added in the revised versions of the EPQ, assesses traits related to aggressiveness, impulsivity, and tough-mindedness. High scores on the psychoticism scale indicate a personality that is more aggressive, unconventional, and less empathetic. Sonic doesn't display many traits associated with psychoticism, as he is typically portrayed as a hero who fights for justice and helps others. His character tends to be empathetic, compassionate, and driven by a strong sense of morality, which makes him low on the psychoticism dimension.
- Lie Scale (L): The Lie Scale is included to identify attempts by respondents to present themselves in a favorable or socially desirable manner. It helps to detect dishonest or exaggerated responses. Sonic doesn't work to make himself look more favorable or socially desirable. He just does what he has to do - so for this scale - let's just say he doesn't exaggerate.

Checking someone's EPQ consists of giving them a series of statements to which respondents provide "yes" or "no" answers. Their responses to these statements are then scored to determine their placement on the extraversion, emotional stability, and, if applicable, psychoticism scales. The Lie Scale is used to assess the accuracy and honesty of the responses. The EPQ has been widely used in research and clinical practice and has been adapted for use in various cultural contexts. It provides a relatively quick and straightforward method for assessing certain aspects of personality. Researchers and clinicians have used it to investigate personality traits, psychological disorders, and other individual differences. Overall, Sonic the Hedgehog's character traits align most closely with the extraversion and emotional stability dimensions of the EPQ. He is an outgoing and adventurous character who maintains emotional stability even in the face of challenges.

WHAT CAN WE LEARN?

While Sonic may experience moments of frustration or anger when faced with particularly vexing challenges, these emotions are usually short-lived and do not define his character. Instead, they serve as temporary fuel to propel him forward. Sonic's resilience, determination, and positive outlook make him a beloved and enduring character who can handle the toughest of trials without being significantly affected psychologically.

THE WITCHER

In "The Witcher," we meet Geralt of Rivia, a skilled monster hunter known as a "Witcher." A Witcher is a profession that involves undergoing mutations and rigorous training to develop superhuman abilities, including enhanced strength, reflexes, and the ability to use magic. Witchers are primarily tasked with hunting and slaying dangerous monsters that threaten the world. Geralt is characterized by his white hair, yellow cat-like eyes, and his signature two swords - a steel one for humans and a silver one for monsters. Geralt's adventures occur in a richly detailed and morally ambiguous fantasy world filled with political intrigue, complex characters, and mythical creatures. He starts searching for his lost memory and becomes embroiled in a complex political conspiracy involving different groups and a mysterious cult. He is later framed for assassination of a king and embarks on a journey to clear his name. Every action can significantly impact his outcome. He later goes on a quest to find his adopted daughter, Ciri, who is pursued by a supernatural force known as the Wild Hunt. Geralt's choices through the morally gray world have consequences, and there is often no clear distinction between good and evil.

CHALLENGES

Geralt faces a multitude of challenges throughout his adventures. These challenges encompass various trials, including combat encounters, moral dilemmas, political intrigue, and personal struggles.

- Monster Hunts: As a Witcher, Geralt's primary occupation is hunting and slaying monsters. These creatures can range from common beasts like wolves and ghouls to more formidable and exotic foes like griffins, wyverns, and vampires. Each monster presents unique challenges, requiring Geralt to adapt his tactics and use his knowledge of the creatures' weaknesses.
- Moral Dilemmas: Geralt often faces difficult choices with no clear right or wrong answers. He encounters situations where he must make decisions that have far-reaching consequences for others around him and the world. These choices can lead to unexpected outcomes and moral quandaries.
- Political Intrigue: The world of The Witcher is filled with political conflicts and power struggles. Geralt often finds himself caught in the midst of these disputes, forced to navigate treacherous political waters and make choices that can shape the fate of nations.
- Personal Quests and Relationships: Geralt is on a personal quest to find his adopted daughter, Ciri, who is pursued by the enigmatic Wild Hunt. He also forms several romantic relationships including Triss Merigold, Yennefer of Vengerberg and others. Balancing these relationships while dealing with the challenges of his profession is complicated.
- Combat Skills and Witcher Signs: Geralt's combat skills and the use of Witcher Signs (simple spells) are essential for surviving battles. He must master these abilities and choose appropriate tactics to defeat different types of enemies.
- Resource Management: Geralt needs to manage resources such as potions, oils, and crafting materials to enhance his combat effectiveness. Careful resource management is crucial for success, especially when facing powerful foes.
- Investigations and Puzzles: Geralt often needs to investigate crime scenes, solve puzzles, and gather clues to progress in his journey.

- Wildlife and Environmental Hazards: The world is teeming with wildlife and environmental hazards that can pose threats to Geralt like treacherous terrain, dealing with weather effects, and surviving in hostile environments.
- Witcher Code: Geralt adheres to a strict code of conduct, which includes avoiding taking sides in political conflicts and remaining neutral. Staying true to this code can be challenging when faced with morally complex decisions.

PSYCHOLOGY

The hardships and challenges that Geralt of Rivia faces throughout The Witcher have a significant impact on his psychology and development. His experiences shape his personality, beliefs, and outlook on the world in several ways:

- Emotional Resilience: Geralt is a character known for his stoicism and emotional restraint. His training as a Witcher and the harsh realities of his profession have conditioned him to remain composed in the face of adversity. This emotional resilience helps him cope with the challenges he encounters.
- Moral Complexity: Geralt's encounters with moral dilemmas and ambiguous choices force him to question his own values and principles. He often has to make difficult decisions that challenge his sense of right and wrong. This moral complexity can lead to introspection and self-reflection.
- Isolation: Witchers are often treated with suspicion and fear by ordinary people because of their mutations and unique abilities. Geralt's status as an outsider and his isolation from society contribute to feelings of alienation and loneliness. His relationships with a select few individuals become even more meaningful as a result.
- Loss and Grief: Geralt experiences loss and grief throughout the series, whether it's losing loved ones or confronting the harsh realities of the world. These experiences can lead to moments of introspection and sadness, contributing to his depth.
- Fatherhood: Geralt's quest to find and protect Ciri introduces him to the role of a father figure. This added responsibility and his emotional connection to Ciri bring out a more nurturing and protective side of his personality. It also adds layers of complexity

to his character as he grapples with the challenges of parenthood.

- Adaptability: Geralt's ability to adapt to different situations and handle various challenges demonstrates his resourcefulness. His willingness to learn, evolve, and change in response to adversity is a testament to his psychological strength.
- Relationships and Trust: The relationships Geralt forms with characters like Triss, Yennefer, and others are deeply affected by the choices he makes. Trust and loyalty become central themes, and Geralt's psychology is influenced by his interactions with these characters.
- Identity: Geralt's identity as a Witcher is a core part of his character, but it's also a source of inner conflict. He grapples with questions of identity, purpose, and belonging as he navigates a world that often sees him as a monster. These struggles add depth to his character psychology.

In summary, Geralt's psychology evolves as he faces and overcomes a wide range of challenges. His emotional resilience, moral complexity, sense of isolation, and evolving relationships with others all contribute to his growth as a character.

THE HUMANISTIC THEORY & GERALT

Humanistic psychology is a psychological perspective that emerged in the mid-20th century as a reaction against the prevailing behaviorist and psychoanalytic approaches. Humanistic psychologists, including Abraham Maslow and Carl Rogers, shifted the focus from studying mental illness and pathology to exploring the positive aspects of human experience, personal growth, and the pursuit of self-actualization. Key principles of Humanistic Theory include:

- Self-Actualization: Central to humanistic psychology is the concept of self-actualization. This is the process of becoming the most that one can be, fulfilling one's potential, and expressing one's unique capabilities. It involves the pursuit of personal goals, meaningful activities, and the development of one's talents. Geralt's journey throughout The Witcher series reflects a quest for self-actualization. He undergoes rigorous training and mutations to become a Witcher, constantly hones his skills, and seeks knowledge about the monsters he hunts. His pursuit of self-improvement and mastery in his profession aligns with the concept of self-actualization.

- Holism: Humanistic psychology emphasizes holism, viewing individuals as whole entities greater than the sum of their parts. This approach considers the interconnectedness of mind, body, and spirit, emphasizing the importance of understanding the person in their entirety rather than focusing solely on specific behaviors or symptoms. Geralt's character is portrayed holistically. He is not merely a monster hunter; he's a complex individual with emotions, relationships, and a moral compass. The interconnectedness of his physical abilities, mental resilience, and emotional experiences contributes to his holistic portrayal.

- Personal Growth and Fulfillment: Humanistic psychologists believe that individuals have an inherent drive toward personal growth and fulfillment. This drive is not only about meeting basic needs but also about reaching higher levels of psychological and emotional well-being. Geralt's character experiences significant personal growth throughout his journey. His encounters with moral dilemmas, complex relationships, and his role as a father figure to Ciri contribute to his journey of personal growth and fulfillment. His choices and actions reflect a desire for a meaningful and fulfilling life.

- Positive Regard and Unconditional Positive Regard: Carl Rogers introduced the concept of positive regard, which is the notion that individuals have an innate need to be accepted, valued, and respected by others. Unconditional positive regard is the acceptance and support of an individual regardless of their behavior. It is a key element in creating an environment conducive to personal growth and self-actualization. Geralt's relationships with characters like Ciri, Yennefer, Triss, and others are central to his story. The importance of these relationships aligns with the humanistic concept of positive regard. Geralt seeks acceptance, understanding, and connection with others, and these relationships play a crucial role in his emotional well-being.

- Self-Concept: The self-concept refers to an individual's perception of themselves, encompassing thoughts, feelings, and beliefs about their own identity and worth. Humanistic psychologists argue that a positive self-concept is crucial for mental health and well-being. Geralt's self-concept is shaped by his experiences as a Witcher and the societal perception of his kind. Despite being an outsider, he maintains a sense of identity and purpose. His self-concept evolves as he forms meaningful relationships and navigates the complexities of the world around him.

- Freedom and Personal Responsibility: Humanistic psychology emphasizes the importance of personal responsibility and freedom of choice. Individuals are seen as active agents in their lives, capable of making meaningful choices that influence their personal development and well-being. Geralt operates in a world filled with moral ambiguity and difficult choices. His ability to make decisions based on his own moral compass and personal responsibility is evident. The freedom to choose his path, even in the face of challenging circumstances, aligns with the humanistic emphasis on personal agency.

- Client-Centered Therapy: Carl Rogers developed client-centered therapy, an approach that places a strong emphasis on the therapeutic relationship and the creation of a safe, non-judgmental space. The therapist provides unconditional positive regard, empathy, and genuine understanding, facilitating the client's self-exploration and personal growth. While not explicitly undergoing therapy, Geralt's interactions with various characters often exhibit elements of client-centered principles. His conversations and relationships reflect empathy, understanding, and the creation of a safe space for emotional expression, particularly in his role as a protector and confidant. Hopefully, they do the same for him.

Humanistic psychology has had a lasting impact on various fields, including psychotherapy, education, and organizational psychology. While it is not as dominant as some other psychological perspectives, its influence can be seen in contemporary approaches that emphasize positive psychology, mindfulness, and a holistic view of human well-being. Geralt of Rivia's character aligns with several key principles of Humanistic Theory. His journey involves self-actualization, personal growth, the pursuit of meaningful relationships, the exploration of freedom and personal responsibility, and the search for meaning in a complex world.

THE LAST OF US

In "The Last of Us" (Naughty Dog, 2013, 2020) the main characters are Joel Miller and Ellie. Joel is a middle-aged, single father living in Texas when a global pandemic strikes, leading to the outbreak of a fungal infection that turns people into violent, zombie-like creatures known as "Clickers." In the chaos, Joel loses his daughter, Sarah, which leaves him emotionally scarred and hardened by the harsh realities of this post-apocalyptic world. He becomes a smuggler and does what it takes to stay alive. He becomes involved in a mission to transport a young girl named Ellie across the country. Ellie is believed to be immune to the infection, and they must reach a group known as the Fireflies, who may be able to find a cure. Joel and Ellie develop a deep and complex father-daughter-like relationship, with Joel serving as Ellie's protector and mentor. Ellie is a resourceful and brave individual who, despite her young age, has learned to navigate the dangers of the post-apocalyptic world. She is both a symbol of hope for a potential cure and a stark reminder of the world's grim reality. The relationship between Joel and Ellie is captivating while they explore elements of love, loss, survival and moral complexities.

CHALLENGES

During their journey, Joel and Ellie face numerous challenges:

- Infected: The most immediate and constant threat is the infected. There are different stages of infection, including Runners, Clickers, and Bloaters, each progressively more dangerous and difficult to deal with. Joel and Ellie must constantly fight or evade these infected creatures as they make their way across the country.
- Hostile Survivors: In addition to the infected, Joel and Ellie often encounter other survivors who may not always have their best interests at heart. Many survivors are willing to do whatever it takes to ensure their own survival, including resorting to violence, theft, and betrayal.
- Scarcity of Resources: Resources such as ammunition, weapons, food, and medical supplies are scarce in the post-apocalyptic world. Joel and Ellie must scavenge for these resources, which can be used for crafting items and healing. Managing their resources effectively is crucial for their survival.
- Environmental Hazards: The world is filled with environmental hazards and traps, including collapsing buildings, hidden mines, and more. Navigating these dangers while avoiding enemies adds an extra layer of challenge to their journey.
- Moral Dilemmas: They encounter many moral dilemmas and complex decisions that have moral and ethical implications. These choices can impact the course of their journey and the characters' relationships.
- Emotional and Psychological Challenges: Both Joel and Ellie carry emotional and psychological burdens from their pasts. Joel grapples with the trauma of losing his daughter, while Ellie faces the weight of being immune to the infection and the consequences of her actions. These emotional challenges are central to the narrative and character development.
- Betrayal and Loss: Throughout their journey, Joel and Ellie experience moments of betrayal and loss, which further test their resilience and trust in others. These experiences shape themselves and their relationships.

Joel and Ellie's lives are challenging and intense. They are in a constant battle for survival and growth while their bond evolves.

PSYCHOLOGY

The hardships and challenges that Joel and Ellie face throughout their journey in "The Last of Us" have a profound impact on their psychology:

Joel Miller:

- Emotional Armor: Joel begins as a hardened and emotionally closed-off individual due to the trauma of losing his daughter during the initial outbreak. He has built emotional walls to protect himself from further pain, which makes it difficult for him to connect with others.
- Protectiveness: Joel's protective instinct, stemming from his guilt over not being able to save his daughter, is directed toward Ellie. As their relationship grows, he becomes fiercely protective of her, often to the point of extreme measures. This protectiveness is both a result of and a response to his past trauma.
- Moral Ambiguity: Over time, Joel's experiences in the harsh post-apocalyptic world led him to make morally ambiguous choices, such as committing acts of violence and deception. He justifies these actions as necessary for survival, reflecting a moral shift brought about by the harsh realities of their world.
- Resistance to Attachment: Joel is initially resistant to forming emotional attachments because of the pain of past losses. However, his growing bond with Ellie challenges this resistance and forces him to confront his feelings.

Ellie:

- Resilience: Ellie, despite her young age, demonstrates remarkable resilience in the face of adversity. She's had to adapt to a world where survival is paramount, and this has made her resourceful and strong-willed.
- Desire for Connection: Ellie's desire for connection and a sense of family is a driving force in her. She lost her parents at a young age and longs for a sense of belonging. This longing is evident in her attachment to Joel.
- Growth and Maturity: Throughout her journey, Ellie matures and becomes more self-reliant. She grapples with her role as a potential savior of humanity due to her immunity and the weight of expectations placed on her.
- Struggles with Violence: Ellie faces internal conflicts regarding the violence she witnesses and partakes in. Her experiences lead

to moments of introspection and questioning the morality of her actions.

- Guilt and Trauma: Ellie carries guilt over the consequences of her choices and actions. This guilt weighs heavily on her throughout the series and contributes to her emotional struggles.

The hardships and challenges they encounter shape Joel and Ellie's psychology in complex ways. While Joel's trauma has led to emotional detachment and moral ambiguity, Ellie's resilience and desire for connection drive her character development.

ATTACHMENT THEORY & ELLIE AND JOEL

Attachment theory is a psychological framework that was developed by John Bowlby, a British psychologist, and later expanded upon by Mary Ainsworth and others. Attachment theory focuses on the bonds and emotional connections formed between individuals, particularly in the context of early caregiver-child relationships. The theory posits that these early attachments have a profound impact on an individual's emotional and social development throughout their life.

Key Concepts of Attachment Theory:

- Attachment: Attachment is the emotional bond or connection formed between an infant and their primary caregiver. This primary caregiver is often the mother, but it can be another consistent and responsive caregiver.
- Attachment Behaviors: Infants display attachment behaviors as a way to seek proximity to their caregiver, especially in times of distress or uncertainty. These behaviors can include crying, smiling, clinging, and reaching out.
- Secure Base: The caregiver serves as a secure base for the child. A secure base is a point of safety and comfort from which the child can explore the world, knowing they can return to the caregiver for support and reassurance.
- Attachment Styles: Attachment theory categorizes individuals into different attachment styles based on their early experiences. The four main attachment styles are:
    - Secure Attachment: Individuals with a secure attachment style typically had caregivers who were responsive, consistent, and nurturing during their childhood. They tend to have positive self-esteem, trust others, and are

comfortable with emotional intimacy in adult relationships. They have a strong sense of self-worth and believe they are worthy of love and care. Children with secure attachment feel confident exploring the world but seek the caregiver for comfort when needed.

- Anxious-Preoccupied Attachment | Insecure-Ambivalent / Resistant Attachment: Individuals with an anxious attachment style often experienced inconsistent caregiving in childhood. They tend to be overly concerned about the availability of their caregivers and may fear rejection or abandonment. In adult relationships, they may exhibit clingy behavior, seek constant reassurance, and worry about the stability of their relationships. Children with insecure-ambivalent attachment may be clingy and hesitant to explore, showing difficulty being soothed.
- Insecure-Avoidant Attachment: Individuals with an avoidant attachment style typically had caregivers who were emotionally distant or inconsistent in their responses. They often develop a self-reliant attitude and an aversion to emotional intimacy. In adult relationships, they may have difficulty expressing their own emotions and may be uncomfortable with emotional closeness. Children with insecure-avoidant attachment may avoid or ignore the caregiver, showing little emotion.
- Insecure-Ambivalent/Resistant Attachment | Disorganized Attachment: This attachment style is characterized by a lack of consistent patterns. Individuals with disorganized attachment often experienced inconsistent or frightening caregiving in childhood. They may struggle with emotional regulation, exhibit erratic behavior, and have difficulty forming stable relationships. This style is marked by inconsistent or unpredictable behaviors, often in response to a caregiver who is frightening or frightened.

- Internal Working Models: Attachment experiences contribute to the development of internal working models - mental representations of the self, others, and relationships. These models influence expectations and behaviors in future relationships.

- Impact on Later Relationships: Attachment theory suggests that the quality of early attachments influences an individual's social and emotional well-being throughout their life. Positive early attachments contribute to the development of secure and healthy relationships, while negative or disrupted attachments can lead to difficulties in forming and maintaining relationships.
- Caregiver Sensitivity: The responsiveness and sensitivity of the caregiver to the child's needs play a crucial role in the formation of secure attachments. A caregiver who consistently meets the child's emotional and physical needs fosters a secure attachment.

Attachment theory has been influential in various fields, including developmental psychology, clinical psychology, and parenting research. It provides a framework for understanding how early experiences shape personality, emotional regulation, and relationship dynamics across the lifespan. The theory is often applied in the study of parent-child relationships, romantic relationships, and therapeutic interventions. If we analyze Joel and Ellie through Attachment Theory, we can observe a few things

- Joel:
    - Secure Base: Joel's early attachment with his daughter Sarah serves as a secure base for understanding his subsequent relationships. The trauma of losing Sarah influences Joel's emotional barriers and reluctance to form new attachments.
    - Fear of Loss: Joel's fear of loss, stemming from the trauma of losing his daughter, is evident in his initial resistance to forming close bonds. This fear may contribute to his protective and sometimes overbearing behavior toward Ellie as he subconsciously seeks to prevent another devastating loss.
    - Emotional Growth: Over the course of their journey, especially in his relationship with Ellie, Joel experiences emotional growth. Ellie becomes a new anchor, a figure he cares deeply for and is willing to protect at all costs.

- Ellie:
    - Lack of Consistent Caregivers: Ellie's early life is marked by the absence of consistent caregivers. The harsh post-apocalyptic world has shaped her into a resilient and self-reliant individual.
    - Desire for Connection: Ellie's longing for connection and a sense of belonging is a central theme. Her attachment to Joel serves as a source of security and emotional support in a world filled with danger and uncertainty.
    - Search for Surrogate Family: Ellie's quest for surrogate family figures, including Joel and others she encounters, reflects her innate need for attachment figures. Her relationships with others, such as Riley, underscore this search for connection.
    - Impact of Loss: Ellie's experiences with loss, including the death of her friend Riley, contribute to her complex attachment dynamics. These losses intensify her desire for meaningful connections and influence her responses to subsequent attachments.

If we analyze Joel and Ellie's relationship through this model we can learn a lot about them. Joel and Ellie are mutually dependent. Joel finds a chance for redemption and emotional healing through this relationship with Ellie, while she gains a sense of security and belonging from her attachment to Joel. The challenges they face together lead to moments of attachment related struggles and growth while they evolve and navigate the complexities of the post-apocalyptic world.

MONKEY ISLAND

Guybrush Threepwood from Monkey Island (LucasArts) is a young and aspiring pirate with a somewhat bumbling and naive personality. His dream is to become a fearsome pirate, and he sets out to accomplish this goal and prove himself. He becomes embroiled in a plot involving the ghost pirate LeChuck, who is in love with the governor of the island, Elaine Marley. Guybrush must rescue Elaine from LeChuck's clutches and ultimately uncover the secret of the mysterious Monkey Island. Guybrush is awkward yet endearing and must navigate through humorous and sometimes absurd situations.

CHALLENGES

Guybrush Threepwood faces numerous challenges and obstacles throughout the Monkey Island series as he embarks on his adventures.

- Pirate Training: He must prove himself as a pirate by completing various tasks, including sword fighting, treasure hunting, and obtaining a crew for a ship.
- Ghost Pirate LeChuck: Throughout his journey, Guybrush faces the recurring antagonist, the ghost pirate LeChuck. LeChuck is a powerful and malevolent foe who constantly thwarts Guybrush's plans and schemes.
- Voodoo and Mysticism: Guybrush often encounters characters skilled in voodoo and mysticism, such as the voodoo priestess,

the Voodoo Lady. He must use his wits and gather ingredients to create voodoo spells and charms to progress in his adventures.

- Puzzle-solving: Guybrush must use items from his inventory and combine them in creative ways to solve various challenges, from escaping a locked room to tricking an enemy.
- Dealing with Odd Characters: Guybrush encounters a wide range of eccentric characters throughout the series, including eccentric shopkeepers, pirates with unusual quirks, and even a group of cannibals. He must navigate these interactions to advance.
- Monkey Island Myths: Guybrush must uncover the secrets and legends surrounding the island, including the elusive "three-headed monkey."
- Time Travel and Confusion: At one point, time travel becomes a central element of the storyline, leading to complex and sometimes confusing challenges as Guybrush tries to set things right.
- Marriage Proposals and Love Interests: Guybrush's love interest, Elaine Marley, frequently finds herself in perilous situations. Guybrush must often rescue her or find ways to win her affection.
- Outlandish Humor: The Monkey Island series is renowned for its zany humor, and many challenges are designed to evoke laughter and amusement as players interact with bizarre characters and situations.

PSYCHOLOGY

Guybrush Threepwood's character is portrayed as an upbeat and optimistic individual throughout the Monkey Island series, and he tends to maintain a cheerful disposition even in the face of adversity. His unwavering determination and often clueless confidence are part of what makes him endearing as a character. However, while Guybrush's psyche remains largely resilient, there are several ways in which the challenges and hardships he faces impact him:

- Growth and Development: Over the course of the series, Guybrush matures and becomes more experienced. While he starts as a bumbling and inexperienced pirate wannabe, he gradually becomes more capable and confident in his abilities. His growth as a character is a result of the challenges he faces and the lessons he learns along the way.

- Frustration and Perseverance: He frequently encounters frustrating and seemingly insurmountable obstacles. While these challenges might cause momentary frustration, they also motivate him to persevere and find creative solutions. This determination to overcome adversity is a defining trait of his character.
- Resilience: Guybrush's resilience is evident in his ability to bounce back from setbacks and failures. Even when his plans go awry, he remains undeterred and continues his quest to achieve his goals, particularly in his pursuit of Elaine Marley's affection.
- Adaptability: Monkey Island often presents him with unexpected and bizarre situations. To succeed, he must adapt quickly and think on his feet. This adaptability becomes a valuable skill as he navigates the unpredictable world.
- Confidence and Self-Esteem: Guybrush's confidence can be bolstered or shaken depending on his choices and the outcomes of his actions. However, his enduring self-belief is a key part of his character, and he typically maintains a positive self-image even when things go wrong.
- Humor as Coping Mechanism: He uses humor as a coping mechanism to deal with the absurdity of his adventures and the challenges he faces. His witty and often self-deprecating humor serves as a way to lighten tense situations and keep his spirits high.
- Relationships: Guybrush's interactions with other characters, particularly his love interest Elaine Marley, play a significant role in his psychological development. His determination to rescue and win Elaine's love drives many of his actions and decisions throughout the series.

POSITIVE PSYCHOLOGY & GUYBRUSH

Positive Psychology is a psychological model and approach that focuses on the study of human well-being, strengths, and positive experiences rather than solely on mental illness or dysfunction. It was developed by Martin Seligman as a reaction to past practices which mainly focused on psychological problems. The theory is built on the humanistic movement by Abraham Maslow, Carl Rogers and Rollo May. It seeks to understand what makes life fulfilling and meaningful, with an emphasis on promoting happiness and flourishing. Here are the key principles and components of Positive Psychology while analyzing Guybrush through them:

- Strengths and Virtues: Positive Psychology identifies various character strengths and virtues, such as courage, kindness, wisdom, and gratitude. It emphasizes the importance of recognizing and cultivating these strengths in individuals. Guybrush exhibits several character strengths that align with the Positive Psychology model. His determination to become a pirate, his unwavering optimism, and his ability to find humor in challenging situations are indicative of strengths like perseverance, optimism, and humor.
- Positive Emotions: This approach emphasizes the role of positive emotions, such as happiness, joy, and contentment, in enhancing well-being. It explores how experiencing positive emotions can lead to greater life satisfaction. Guybrush consistently experiences positive emotions, even in the face of adversity. His humor and upbeat outlook serve as coping mechanisms and contribute to his overall well-being.
- Subjective Well-Being: Positive Psychology considers subjective well-being, which includes life satisfaction, happiness, and overall positive feelings about life, as a central component of psychological health. Throughout his journey, Guybrush's ultimate goal is to achieve happiness and fulfillment, whether it's by becoming a pirate or winning the love of Elaine. His journey and adventures are driven by a desire for personal well-being and satisfaction.
- Resilience: This examines how individuals can develop resilience, the ability to bounce back from adversity, and how this resilience can contribute to overall well-being. Guybrush repeatedly faces setbacks and obstacles, but he always bounces back with determination. His resilience in the face of LeChuck's threats and the bizarre challenges on Monkey Island showcases his ability to overcome adversity.
- Meaning and Purpose: Positive Psychology explores the importance of having a sense of meaning and purpose in life, as it can lead to a greater sense of fulfillment. Guybrush's pursuit of his dreams, such as becoming a pirate or saving Elaine, provides him with a sense of meaning and purpose in his adventures.

These goals give his life direction and contribute to his sense of fulfillment.

Guybrush can be analyzed through the Positive Psychology model as a character who embodies several key elements of well-being and positive psychology. His strengths, resilience, humor, and pursuit of happiness make him a compelling example of how positive psychology principles can manifest in a person's journey and personality.

WHAT CAN WE LEARN?

Overall, while Guybrush Threepwood faces a wide array of hardships and challenges in Monkey Island, his character remains resilient and optimistic. His ability to adapt, persevere, and find humor in even the most dire circumstances are central to his character's charm.

UNCHARTED

The main character in the Naughty Dog Uncharted series is Nathan "Nate" Drake. Drake is a charismatic and adventurous treasure hunter who's often witty, resourceful, and often roguish. He is a skilled marksman, climber, and explorer. Nate has a deep knowledge of history and archaeology, which he uses to hunt for lost and legendary treasures. He is often accompanied by a diverse cast of characters, including his mentor Victor "Sully" Sullivan and love interest Elena Fisher. At the beginning, he sets out to find the lost treasure of El Dorado. He heads out to a mysterious island in the Pacific, where he faces mercenaries and uncovers a dark secret. Later, Nate is drawn into a race to find Marco Polo's lost fleet and the mythical city of Shambhala. After that, he goes on a search for the "Atlantis of the Sands" in the Arabian desert. And if that is not enough - he later searches for the pirate colony of Libertalia, facing off against a rival treasure hunter, Rafe Adler. His journeys explore themes of loyalty, morality, and the cost of adventure.

CHALLENGES

Throughout his journeys, Nate faces a multitude of challenges and obstacles:

- Environmental Hazards: He often finds himself in perilous environments that test his climbing, navigation, and survival skills. These include treacherous cliffs, collapsing structures, and challenging terrain.

- Puzzle-Solving: Nate must solve intricate puzzles and riddles, many of which are tied to the historical mysteries and treasures he seeks and must decipher clues, manipulate ancient mechanisms, and solve complex puzzles to progress.
- Combat: He encounters a wide range of adversaries, including mercenaries, pirates, and other treasure hunters. Combat requires him to use cover, engage in gunfights, and employ stealth tactics to defeat enemies.
- Exploration: Much of his journey involves exploring exotic and dangerous locales, from lush jungles to ancient ruins. Nate must navigate through these environments while uncovering secrets and hidden passages.
- Platforming: He frequently engages in platforming and acrobatic maneuvers as he jumps across gaps, swings on ropes, and scales walls. Precise timing and quick reflexes are essential to succeed in these sequences. Practice makes perfect.
- Survival: Survival is a recurring theme, especially in the face of natural disasters or unexpected events. Nate must escape from collapsing buildings, sinking ships, and other life-threatening situations.
- Treacherous Foes: He has many memorable antagonists who pose significant challenges. These foes often have complex motivations and personalities, making confrontations with them more intense.
- Moral Dilemmas: Nate faces moral dilemmas that force him to make choices that can affect his outcome. These dilemmas add depth to the narrative and reflect on his character.
- Character Relationships: Nate's relationships with other characters, such as Sully and Elena, are central. Challenges often arise from conflicts or dilemmas within these relationships.
- History and Mythology: Nate's adventures are deeply intertwined with historical mysteries and myths, and he must navigate the complexities of deciphering ancient texts, artifacts, and legends to uncover the truth.
- Time Pressure: Many times, there is a sense of urgency and time pressure as he races against rivals or impending disasters to secure the treasure.

These challenges combine to create a sense of excitement, danger, and adventure that defines Uncharted and Nate. He must use his problem-solving abilities, combat skills, and knowledge of history to overcome these obstacles and uncover the hidden treasures and secrets of the past.

PSYCHOLOGY

Throughout the Uncharted series, Nathan Drake faces a wide range of hardships and challenges that have a significant impact on his psychology and character development. These challenges shape him into a complex and resilient individual but also take a toll on his mental and emotional well-being. Here's how these hardships affect his psychology:

- Desensitization to Violence: Over time, Nate becomes increasingly desensitized to violence. He starts as a relatively mild-mannered treasure hunter but is forced to confront and kill numerous adversaries. This transformation can lead to moral dilemmas and internal conflicts as he grapples with the necessity of violence for survival.
- Survival Instincts: The constant peril and life-threatening situations he encounters force him to develop strong survival instincts. He becomes highly adaptable, resourceful, and capable of making quick decisions under extreme pressure. His heightened awareness and ability to adapt contribute to his survival.
- Resilience: Nate's resilience is tested repeatedly as he faces seemingly insurmountable odds, narrowly escapes death, and navigates treacherous environments. His ability to bounce back from adversity and persevere in the face of danger becomes a defining trait.
- Psychological Toll: The intense experiences he goes through take a psychological toll on him. He endures trauma, stress, and constant danger, which can lead to symptoms such as anxiety, insomnia, and post-traumatic stress. These psychological effects are evident in his character throughout the series.
- Moral Complexity: Nate grapples with moral complexity as he balances his desire for treasure and adventure with the consequences of his actions. His choices often have ethical implications, and he must confront the moral gray areas of his adventures.

- Conflict and Trust Issues: His relationships with other characters are often strained due to the dangers he exposes them to. He struggles with trust issues, fearing that his actions could endanger those he cares about. This can lead to tension and conflict within his relationships.
- Addiction to Adventure: Nate's pursuit of treasure and adventure can be seen as an addiction. He is drawn to the thrill and excitement of his dangerous lifestyle, and this addiction can negatively impact his personal life and relationships.
- Loss and Grief: He experiences significant losses throughout the series, including the deaths of friends and allies. These losses weigh heavily on him, and he must cope with grief while continuing his adventures.
- Character Evolution: Nate's character undergoes significant growth and development over the course of the series. He evolves from a cocky and reckless adventurer into a more mature and introspective individual who recognizes the costs and consequences of his actions.

The hardships and challenges he faces in "Uncharted" deeply affect his psychology and character. While they contribute to his resilience, resourcefulness, and personal growth, they also bring about psychological stress, moral dilemmas, and complex emotional responses. These elements make Nathan Drake a multi-dimensional and relatable man.

SOCIAL COGNITIVE THEORY & NATE

Albert Bandura's Social Cognitive Theory is a comprehensive framework that emphasizes the role of observational learning, imitation, and social influence in shaping human behavior. His framework includes:

- Observational Learning: involves acquiring new behaviors or information by watching others. Individuals can learn by observing the consequences of others' actions and adjusting their behavior accordingly. For Nate, this is evident in his mentorship under Victor "Sully" Sullivan. Nate learns valuable skills, problem-solving strategies, and the adventurous mindset by observing and modeling Sully's behavior.
- Modeling: refers to the process of imitating the behavior of others. Individuals often look to role models for guidance and

may replicate observed behaviors in similar situations. Nate serves as a model for others in Uncharted. His actions, decisions, and problem-solving methods are observed and, in some cases, replicated by those around him. Additionally, Nate often encounters both positive and negative role models during his adventures, impacting his choices and development.

- Self-Efficacy: is the belief in one's own ability to succeed in specific situations or accomplish particular tasks. Bandura emphasizes the role of self-efficacy in motivation and behavior. Nate's confidence in navigating dangerous environments, solving intricate puzzles, and outsmarting adversaries reflects high self-efficacy. This belief in his own competence contributes to his resilience and determination.

- Reciprocal Determinism: posits that personal factors, behavior, and the environment interact and influence each other in a dynamic manner. Bandura highlights the bidirectional relationship between these three components. Nate's behavior is shaped by his personal characteristics (e.g., adventurous nature), his interactions with the environment (e.g., dangerous landscapes), and the feedback he receives from others (e.g., positive reinforcement or punishment).

- Vicarious Reinforcement and Punishment: occur when individuals experience the consequences (positive or negative) of others' behaviors, influencing their own motivations and actions. The rewards Nate gains from successful treasure hunting, the satisfaction of solving puzzles, and the positive reinforcement from allies contribute to his motivation. Conversely, the dangers he faces, losses he endures, and potential negative consequences serve as forms of vicarious punishment.

- Cognitive Processes, including attention, perception, memory, and problem-solving, play a central role in Bandura's theory. Individuals process information, interpret cues, and apply cognitive skills to guide their behavior. Nate's cognitive processes, including perception, attention, memory, and problem-solving, are central to his success. His ability to assess and interpret his surroundings, remember historical and archaeological information, and devise strategies reflects the cognitive aspects of Bandura's theory.

- Social Modeling and Imitation: involves observing and imitating the behaviors of others. Role models influence individuals' actions, attitudes, and choices. Nate's actions are influenced by the characters around him, such as Sully, Elena, and other allies. Social modeling and imitation are evident as Nate incorporates elements of others' behavior into his own repertoire.

Albert Bandura's Social Cognitive Theory has had a significant impact on the field of psychology, especially in understanding how social influences and observational learning shape human behavior. The theory has practical applications in fields such as education, therapy, and media studies, highlighting the importance of role models, observational learning, and cognitive processes in human development and behavior.

SIMON THE SORCERER

In "Simon the Sorcerer" (1993, Adventure Soft), Simon is a teenage boy who is transported into a magical world through a portal in his bathroom. He's a bit of a smart aleck, often making sarcastic remarks, and he's not particularly enthusiastic about doing chores or dealing with everyday problems. One day, while tasked with doing chores and cleaning the bathroom, he discovers a portal on the floor that leads to another world filled with wizards, talking animals, and fantastical creatures. In this new world, he quickly learns that he's not just an ordinary teenager but the "Chosen One" destined to save the realm from an evil sorcerer named Sordid. Simon's journey in this magical world is filled with humorous and challenging adventures. Along the way, he encounters quirky characters, solves puzzles, and gains magical abilities. Simon's interactions with the inhabitants of the magical world are often clever and witty, and his sarcastic personality provides much humor. As Simon progresses, he unravels the mysteries of this fantasy realm, collects items, and tries to thwart Sordid's evil plans.

CHALLENGES

Simon faces various challenges and obstacles as he embarks on his adventure in the magical world.

- Puzzles: Simon must solve various puzzles, including logic, inventory, and riddles. He must use his wits to collect and combine items, manipulate objects, and decipher clues.
- Navigating the Magical World: He navigates through various locations, such as forests, castles, and dungeons. Finding the right path and avoiding dangerous creatures and traps is a recurring challenge.
- Interacting with Quirky Characters: Throughout his journey, Simon encounters a wide array of eccentric and humorous characters. These characters often engage in witty and comical dialogues, and he must tread carefully and choose the right responses or actions to progress and obtain essential information.
- Gaining Magical Abilities: As Simon's adventure progresses, he gains access to magical abilities and spells. Learning how to use these abilities effectively and at the right moments is crucial for overcoming certain obstacles and defeating enemies.
- Collecting Items: Along his journey, he must collect various items, including magical artifacts, potions, and everyday objects. These items are often essential for solving puzzles or advancing in his journey.
- Confronting Sordid's Minions: Sordid, the main antagonist, has sent his minions to thwart Simon's progress. Simon must find creative ways to deal with these minions and thwart Sordid's plans.
- Navigating Time and Space: Sometimes, he needs to manipulate time or travel through different dimensions to solve puzzles or reach specific locations. These challenges add an extra layer of complexity to the puzzles.
- Understanding the Rules of the Fantasy World: Since Simon comes from the real world, he often has to adapt to the rules and logic of the magical realm. Understanding how magic works and adapting to the fantastical environment is a recurring challenge.

PSYCHOLOGY

The hardships and challenges that Simon faces on his journey through the magical world can have several effects on his psychology and personality:

- Adaptation to a New Reality: Initially, Simon is a typical teenager from the real world, and the sudden transition to a fantastical realm can be disorienting and overwhelming. This dramatic change in environment and circumstances can lead to confusion and a sense of disconnection from his familiar reality.
- Frustration and Resilience: Simon encounters numerous puzzles and obstacles that require him to think creatively and persistently. Failing to solve a puzzle or facing setbacks in his quest may lead to frustration. However, overcoming these challenges can also build resilience as Simon learns to adapt and persevere.
- Development of Problem-Solving Skills: As Simon navigates the magical world and solves complex puzzles, he gains problem-solving skills. This can boost his confidence and sense of competence, leading to a more positive psychological outlook.
- Exposure to Eccentric Characters: Interacting with the magical world's eccentric and often comical characters can lead to a range of emotions, from amusement to annoyance. These interactions may influence Simon's psychological state, especially given his sarcastic nature.
- Sarcasm as a Coping Mechanism: His sarcastic personality is one of his defining traits. It serves as a coping mechanism and a way to handle the absurdity and challenges he encounters. Sarcasm can be a defense mechanism to mask his insecurities or discomfort in the new world.
- Increased Confidence: During his adventure, Simon gains magical abilities and becomes more confident in his role as the "Chosen One." This newfound confidence can positively impact his self-esteem and sense of purpose.
- Psychological Resilience: His ability to adapt to a completely unfamiliar and often whimsical world demonstrates a level of psychological resilience. Despite the challenges, he continues to pursue his quest to thwart Sordid's evil plans.

SOCIAL LEARNING THEORY & SIMON

Social Learning Theory, also developed by psychologist Albert Bandura and modified by many others (Miller, Dollard, Rotter, Burgess and Akers), is a psychological framework that emphasizes the role of observational learning, modeling and reinforcement in shaping human behavior. The theory posits that individuals can learn new behaviors and attitudes by observing the actions of others and the consequences of those actions. Let's explore Social Learning Theory and analyze Simon from "Simon the Sorcerer" through this lens:

- Observational Learning: Social Learning Theory strongly emphasizes the process of observational learning, where individuals learn by watching others. This includes the acquisition of new behaviors, skills, and knowledge through observation. Throughout his journey, Simon engages in observational learning by closely observing the behaviors of other characters in the magical world. For example, he learns how to cast spells, solve puzzles, and interact with magical creatures by watching and imitating the actions of wizards and other inhabitants.

- Modeling: Modeling involves imitating the behaviors of role models or significant others. The model's behavior can serve as a guide for the observer, influencing their own behavior. Bandura's Bobo Doll Experiment where children imitated aggressive behavior is a classic example of modeling in the context of aggression. Simon's behavior is influenced by the modeling of characters he encounters on his journey. Positive role models, such as helpful wizards and friendly creatures, inspire him to adopt certain behaviors and attitudes. Conversely, negative models, such as Sordid and his minions, serve as examples of behaviors to avoid.

- Reinforcement: According to Social Learning Theory, reinforcement plays a crucial role in the learning process. Positive reinforcement (reward) or negative reinforcement (removing a negative consequence) can strengthen the likelihood of a behavior being repeated. For Simon, successfully solving puzzles, achieving milestones, and progressing in the quest provide positive reinforcement for his actions. On the other hand, facing consequences for poor decisions or failing certain tasks is a form of feedback.

- Vicarious Reinforcement: Individuals can also be influenced by observing the consequences of others' actions. If a person sees someone being rewarded or punished for a particular behavior, they may adjust their own behavior based on these observed consequences. Simon witnesses the consequences of others' actions in the magical world. For instance, he may observe characters being rewarded for their kindness or punished for their misdeeds. These observed consequences can influence Simon's own choices and behavior.

- Self-Efficacy: Bandura introduced the concept of self-efficacy, which refers to an individual's belief in their ability to perform a specific task or achieve a particular goal. High self-efficacy is associated with increased motivation and persistence. Simon's self-efficacy undergoes development as he gains experience and confidence in his abilities. Initially unsure of his role as the "Chosen One," he becomes more self-assured as he successfully tackles challenges, learns new skills, and progresses in his quest.

Social Learning Theory provides a framework for understanding how Simon learns, adapts, and develops throughout his journey, which involves observational learning, modeling, and reinforcement, with the various characters and events in the magical world shaping his behavior and contributing to his growth as a character.

RESIDENT EVIL

One of the most iconic and recurring characters in "Resident Evil" is Chris Redfield. As a member of the Special Tactics and Rescue Service (STARS), a police unit in Raccoon City, he and his team are sent to investigate mysterious events at the Arklay Mansion, which leads to their encounter with zombies and other biological horrors created by the Umbrella Corporation. Later on, Chris continues to investigate the Umbrella Corporation and its nefarious activities while searching for his sister, Claire Redfield, who Umbrella has captured. He also plays a significant role in partnering up with Sheva Alomar to investigate a bioterrorist threat in Africa. At this time, Chris delves into his past and history with the series' main antagonist, Albert Wesker. Later on, in a more militaristic role, while helping Ethan Winters, he leads his team to counter a new bioterror threat posed by the mysterious figure, Mother Miranda.

CHALLENGES

Chris Redfield faces various challenges, reflecting the intense and often terrifying nature of his journey. These challenges include:

- Bioterrorist Threats: He frequently confronts bioterrorist threats involving dangerous viruses and bio-organic weapons. These threats are often engineered by organizations seeking to use viral outbreaks as a means of achieving their sinister goals.

- Mutated Creatures: Chris encounters many mutated and bioengineered creatures, including zombies, B.O.W.s (Bio Organic Weapons), and other monstrous entities. These creatures are the result of experiments with the T-virus, G-virus, and other viral agents.
- Personal Loss: Chris experiences personal loss and the deaths of comrades, friends, and family members. The emotional toll of these losses adds depth to his character and motivates him to continue his fight against bioterrorism.
- Betrayals and Deceptions: Throughout the series, he faces betrayals and deceptions from individuals he once trusted. Notably, his encounters with Albert Wesker, a former ally turned antagonist, involve complex personal and professional conflicts.
- Global Scale Threats: Sometimes, Chris deals with threats on a global scale. The bioterrorism crises he faces have widespread implications, requiring him to navigate complex situations involving international conspiracies and multiple adversaries.
- Moral Ambiguity: He often grapples with moral ambiguity and ethical dilemmas. The series explores the consequences of bioengineering and the questionable actions of corporations and individuals involved in these experiments.
- Haunted Environments: The settings in which Chris operates, such as eerie mansions, abandoned facilities, and post-apocalyptic landscapes, create an atmospheric challenge. These environments are filled with puzzles, traps, and horrific surprises.
- Personal Struggles: Chris undergoes personal struggles, including his quest to rescue his sister Claire, as well as internal conflicts regarding his role in bioterrorism prevention and the repercussions of his past decisions.
- Physical and Mental Stress: The constant battles and life-threatening situations subject him to significant physical and mental stress. This includes facing powerful adversaries and overcoming overwhelming odds in combat.
- Puzzles and Obstacles: To progress, Chris must solve or navigate intricate puzzles and obstacles. These challenges add an element of strategy and critical thinking.
- The Molded: At one point, he faces a new type of bioweapon known as the Molded. These creatures are part of a new viral

threat, and he must navigate the dangers they pose in a decrepit mansion.

- Leadership Responsibilities: As a leader within organizations like S.T.A.R.S. and the B.S.A.A., Chris assumes significant leadership responsibilities. This involves making tough decisions, coordinating teams, and ensuring the safety of those under his command.

Overall, Chris Redfield's challenges are multifaceted, ranging from immediate physical threats to complex moral dilemmas. His resilience and determination to overcome these challenges are central to his character in the Resident Evil series.

PSYCHOLOGY

As you can see, Chris Redfield faces numerous hardships and life-threatening situations that undoubtedly have a profound impact on his psychology and character. There are several ways in which these challenges affect Chris:

- Post-Traumatic Stress Disorder (PTSD): Chris repeatedly encounters terrifying scenarios, including zombie outbreaks, mutant creatures, and betrayals by people he once trusted. These traumatic experiences can lead to symptoms of PTSD, such as flashbacks, nightmares, and heightened anxiety. Although we don't explicitly delve into his mental state, it's reasonable to assume that Chris would suffer from some level of psychological trauma.
- Survivor's Guilt: He often loses friends and allies in his missions, and he may experience survivor's guilt, a feeling of responsibility for the deaths of those he couldn't save. This guilt can lead to emotional distress and a sense of personal failure.
- Distrust and Paranoia: Given the numerous betrayals and hidden agendas he encounters, Chris may develop a sense of distrust and paranoia towards others. This is especially evident in his interactions with Albert Wesker, a former ally turned antagonist who repeatedly manipulates and deceives him.
- Obsession with Stopping Umbrella: His relentless pursuit of the Umbrella Corporation, the source of many of the bioterrorism threats, could be seen as an obsession. This single-minded focus

on taking down Umbrella might affect his personal relationships and mental well-being.

- Resilience and Determination: On the positive side, Chris's experiences also contribute to his resilience and determination. He repeatedly faces overwhelming odds and dangerous situations but continues to fight for the greater good, and this resilience is a defining trait of his character.
- Leadership and Responsibility: He often finds himself in leadership roles, whether it's leading his STARS team or partnering with others in crises. This can lead to feelings of responsibility for the safety of his team members and civilians, further adding to his psychological burden.
- Emotional Stoicism: Chris is typically portrayed as emotionally stoic, focusing on the mission at hand rather than expressing his feelings openly. This emotional suppression could be a coping mechanism developed over time to deal with the constant horrors he encounters.

LOGOTHERAPY & CHRIS

Logotherapy is a psychotherapeutic approach developed by Viktor Frankl, an Austrian neurologist, psychiatrist, and Holocaust survivor. Frankl founded logotherapy based on his experiences in Nazi concentration camps and his observations of how individuals coped with extreme suffering and adversity. The central premise of logotherapy is the pursuit of meaning as the primary motivational force in human life. Key principles of logotherapy include:

- Search for Meaning: Frankl proposed that the primary driving force in human existence is the search for meaning. He argued that individuals are motivated to find purpose and significance in their lives, even while suffering. Chris Redfield's character consistently faces extreme adversity, including bioterrorism threats, mutated creatures, and personal losses. Despite these challenges, Chris remains dedicated to combating bioterrorism, protecting others, and seeking justice. His commitment to a higher purpose and the well-being of humanity reflects a search for meaning amid adversity.
- Will to Meaning: Logotherapy emphasizes the "will to meaning" as a fundamental aspect of human nature. Frankl asserted that

individuals can find meaning in all aspects of life, including suffering, by adopting a positive attitude and a sense of responsibility for one's own choices and actions. Chris's character exemplifies this will to meaning through his unwavering dedication to his mission. Whether leading his team, confronting powerful adversaries, or navigating complex moral dilemmas, Chris consistently demonstrates a strong sense of purpose.

- Freedom of Will: Logotherapy acknowledges the human capacity for freedom of will. Even in challenging circumstances, individuals have the power to choose their responses and attitudes. This freedom allows individuals to find meaning in their lives. Despite the horrors he faces, Chris's character has the freedom to choose his responses. Whether in moments of crisis or during personal losses, his choices reflect his commitment to his values and the pursuit of a meaningful life.

- Triadic Model: Frankl introduced a triadic model to describe the dynamics of human existence. The model consists of the dimensions of experience: the individual, the world, and meaning. The interplay among these dimensions influences a person's psychological well-being. Chris's character interacts with a world filled with bioterrorist threats and mutated creatures. Through his actions and choices, he seeks to create meaning by combating these threats and protecting others, contributing to the world's well-being and affirming his own sense of purpose.

- Existential Vacuum: Frankl described the concept of an "existential vacuum," a condition in which individuals experience a sense of emptiness and meaninglessness. This vacuum may arise when individuals fail to find or create meaning in their lives. While Chris faces overwhelming challenges, he actively engages in the pursuit of meaning. The absence of an existential vacuum in his character is evident in his proactive approach to combating bioterrorism and the dedication he demonstrates in the face of adversity.

- Paradoxical Intention: Logotherapy employs the technique of paradoxical intention, encouraging individuals to confront their fears or anxieties by deliberately engaging in behaviors that counter those fears. This technique aims to help individuals overcome psychological obstacles. While this specific technique may not be directly applicable to Chris's character, his consistent willingness to confront formidable adversaries and face dangers head-on aligns with the idea of overcoming obstacles through intentional action.

- Dereflection: Dereflection involves shifting one's focus away from excessive self-awareness or self-centeredness by redirecting attention toward meaningful goals and values. This technique can be beneficial for individuals struggling with obsessive thoughts or anxieties. Chris's ability to remain focused on the mission, fulfill leadership responsibilities, and prioritize the well-being of others reflects a form of deflection that contributes to his resilience in the face of existential challenges and adversity.

Logotherapy is applied in clinical practice to help individuals overcome a variety of psychological challenges, including anxiety, depression, and existential crises. Therapists working within the framework of logotherapy often guide individuals in exploring their values, identifying sources of meaning, and fostering a sense of purpose in their lives. Analyzing Chris Redfield through logotherapy highlights his resilience, commitment to a higher purpose, and his ongoing search for meaning in a world filled with bioterrorism and existential threats. His character embodies many aspects of Viktor Frankl's existential philosophy, emphasizing the significance of purpose and choice in the face of adversity.

METAL GEAR SOLID

One of the most iconic and central characters in Metal Gear Solid (Hideo Kojima) is Solid Snake. Solid Snake, whose real name is David, is a genetically enhanced soldier and covert operative. His journey is complex and spans several decades, involving a mix of political intrigue, military conflicts, and the use of advanced technology. At the beginning, he is tasked with infiltrating a nuclear weapons facility called Shadow Moses Island to thwart a terrorist plot led by his genetic twin brother, Liquid Snake. Snake must also confront his past and the shadowy organization known as FOXHOUND. Later on in life, suffering from accelerated aging due to his genetic modifications, in a world filled with private military companies, he's on a quest to uncover the truth about his past and the conspiracy surrounding him. Solid Snake is known for his stealth skills, combat expertise, and strong sense of duty. His character undergoes significant development as he grapples with the consequences of his actions, questions his identity, and faces the moral complexities of the world he operates in.

CHALLENGES

Solid Snake faces a wide range of challenges and obstacles throughout his adventures. These challenges are often physical and moral in nature and test Snake's skills, resolve, and principles.

- Stealth and Infiltration: Snake is often tasked with infiltrating heavily fortified enemy facilities, and stealth is paramount. He must avoid detection by guards, security systems, and surveillance cameras. This requires patience, cunning, and careful planning.

- Combat: While Snake is a highly trained soldier, he frequently finds himself outnumbered and outgunned. He must use his combat skills, various weapons, and tactics to overcome armed adversaries and formidable bosses.

- Moral Dilemmas: The Metal Gear Solid series delves into complex moral and philosophical themes. Snake often grapples with decisions that challenge his sense of right and wrong, such as whether to take a life, the consequences of his actions, and the ethics of warfare.

- Emotional Struggles: Snake's character is marked by emotional turmoil. He battles with the burden of his genetic heritage, the weight of his past deeds, and the knowledge that his actions have far-reaching consequences for the world.

- Betrayal and Deception: Snake frequently encounters characters who are not what they seem, leading to betrayals and shifting alliances. He must navigate a web of deceit and espionage to uncover the truth.

- Advanced Technology: The Metal Gear world features futuristic technology and weapons, including bipedal nuclear-armed mechs called Metal Gears. Snake must confront and neutralize these technological threats, often using unconventional methods.

- Environmental Hazards: In addition to human adversaries, Snake must contend with environmental challenges such as extreme weather conditions, hazardous terrain, and traps set by enemies.

- Time Constraints: In some missions, Snake is under time pressure, adding an extra layer of tension and urgency to his tasks.

- Mental and Physical Strain: Snake's genetic enhancements come at a cost, and he suffers from physical and mental stress, including accelerated aging. Managing his health and well-being becomes a challenge later on.
- Conspiracy and Political Intrigue: The Metal Gear Solid world is known for its intricate and convoluted situations involving government conspiracies, shadowy organizations, and geopolitical maneuvering. Snake must uncover these secrets while navigating a web of political intrigue.

Throughout these challenges, Snake's resilience, resourcefulness, and determination shine through. His character development is a central aspect of the series, as he faces these trials and evolves as a character, ultimately contributing to the complexity and depth of the Metal Gear Solid narrative.

PSYCHOLOGY

The hardships and challenges Solid Snake faces have a profound impact on his psychology and character development. Snake's psychological struggles are a central theme in the series, contributing to his complex and multi-dimensional personality.

- Post-Traumatic Stress: Snake repeatedly experiences traumatic events, including combat, betrayal, and witnessing the consequences of war. These experiences lead to symptoms of post-traumatic stress disorder (PTSD), such as flashbacks, nightmares, and emotional numbness. Snake becomes haunted by the memories of his past missions and the violence he has witnessed.
- Existential Angst: Snake often grapples with existential questions about his identity, purpose, and the morality of his actions. He questions the significance of his existence, given his role as a soldier and the seemingly endless cycle of conflict.
- Isolation and Loneliness: Snake's life is marked by isolation and loneliness. He frequently operates alone, cut off from close human connections, which contributes to feelings of alienation and detachment.
- Cynicism and Distrust: Due to his experiences with betrayal and deception, Snake becomes increasingly cynical and distrustful of authority figures and organizations. He learns to question the

motives of those around him and is often hesitant to form emotional bonds.

- Moral Conflicts: Snake faces moral dilemmas that challenge his sense of right and wrong. He must make difficult decisions, such as taking lives, to achieve his mission objectives. These moral conflicts weigh heavily on his conscience and lead to inner turmoil.
- Desire for Redemption: As his life progresses, Snake seeks redemption for his past actions and the legacy of his genetic lineage. He strives to make amends for the destruction caused by the Metal Gear program and the conflicts he has been involved in.
- Physical Decline: Snake's accelerated aging due to genetic modifications is a constant reminder of his mortality. His physical decline adds an additional layer of psychological stress as he grapples with his own mortality and the limited time he has left.
- Loss of Innocence: Throughout the series, Snake witnesses the horrors of war and the human cost of conflict. This loss of innocence and exposure to the darker aspects of humanity deeply affects his worldview and contributes to his psychological struggles.
- Identity Crisis: Snake's identity is deeply entwined with his role as a soldier. As he questions the purpose of his existence, he also grapples with the question of whether he can ever truly escape his past and find a new identity beyond being a warrior.
- Emotional Resilience: Despite the psychological toll of his experiences, Snake demonstrates remarkable emotional resilience and determination. He continues to push forward and confront his demons, showing a willingness to confront his inner struggles.

Solid Snake's psychological journey is a central element, adding depth and complexity to his character. It also serves as a vehicle for exploring profound themes of war, technology, ethics, and the human condition.

THE PTSD MODEL & SOLID SNAKE

Post-Traumatic Stress Disorder (PTSD) is a mental health condition that can develop in individuals who have experienced or witnessed a traumatic event. PTSD can result from a variety of traumatic experiences, such as combat exposure, sexual assault, natural disasters, serious accidents, or witnessing violence. Certain risk factors, including a history of trauma, pre-existing mental health conditions, and lack of a strong support system, can increase the likelihood of developing PTSD. The disorder is characterized by a range of symptoms that can persist long after the traumatic event has occurred. The symptoms are generally categorized into four clusters:

- Intrusive Thoughts and Memories: Individuals with PTSD often experience intrusive, distressing thoughts, memories, or flashbacks related to the traumatic event. These can be triggered by various stimuli and lead to emotional distress. Throughout the Metal Gear Solid series, Snake encounters traumatic events, including intense combat situations, betrayal, and the consequences of warfare. His experiences may lead to intrusive memories and flashbacks, impacting his mental well-being.

- Avoidance: People with PTSD may avoid reminders of the traumatic event, including places, people, or activities that trigger distressing memories. Avoidance is a coping mechanism aimed at preventing the re-experiencing of trauma. Snake exhibits a degree of avoidance in his interactions with others and the avoidance of revisiting certain locations that hold traumatic memories. This behavior is consistent with the avoidance seen in individuals with PTSD.

- Negative Alterations in Cognitions and Mood: PTSD can lead to negative changes in a person's thought patterns and emotional states. This may include persistent negative beliefs about oneself, others, or the world and a persistent negative emotional state. Snake's character undergoes significant emotional and psychological challenges, and he grapples with questions of morality, purpose, and the consequences of his actions. His negative thoughts and emotional struggles align with this aspect of PTSD.

- Hyperarousal and Reactivity: Individuals with PTSD may experience heightened arousal and reactivity, including irritability, difficulty sleeping, and being easily startled. These symptoms are indicative of a heightened "fight or flight" response. Snake's character often operates in high-stress environments, and his heightened vigilance, combat readiness, and occasional signs of irritability are consistent with the hyperarousal seen in PTSD.

- Duration and Impact: For a diagnosis of PTSD, these symptoms must persist for more than one month and cause significant impairment in social, occupational, or other important areas of functioning. The symptoms often cause significant distress, affecting the individual's overall quality of life.

Snake's character exhibits behaviours that align with some aspects of PTSD; the application of the PTSD model to Snake is a way to interpret his character through a psychological lens, recognizing the symbolic nature of his experiences.

DEVIL MAY CRY

Dante, a skilled and cocky demon hunter with a devil-may-care attitude, a love for pizza, and distinctive white hair and red coat, is the main character in Devil May Cry. He is also a half-demon, as his father, Sparda, was a powerful demon who turned against his own kind to protect humanity, and his mother was a human. Dante's past includes a complicated relationship with his twin brother, Vergil, whom he rebelled against in his quest for power. Throughout his journey, Dante takes on various demon-related jobs and uncovers a conspiracy involving the demon emperor Mundus while exploring his heritage and his desire to avenge his mother's death. Later, Dante is tasked with stopping a businessman named Arius, who aims to obtain great demonic power. At one point during his journey, Dante helps out Nero, a young demon hunter, when he confronts the Order of the Sword, a religious organization with sinister plans. After that, he goes up against the demon king Urizen and continues to battle against demonic forces, exploring his relationship with his family. Throughout his journey, Dante's character is defined by his confident and laid-back demeanor, exceptional combat skills, and ongoing quest to protect humanity from demonic threats while dealing with his own internal struggles and his father's legacy.

CHALLENGES

Dante faces numerous challenges and obstacles throughout his journey. These challenges typically involve battling powerful demons and supernatural forces, uncovering dark conspiracies, and dealing with personal dilemmas.

- Battling Powerful Demons: His primary role as a demon hunter involves taking on some of the most powerful and menacing demons and supernatural creatures. These adversaries test his combat skills, reflexes, and strategic thinking.
- Uncovering Dark Conspiracies: his journey is filled with secret organizations, corrupt individuals, and hidden agendas. Dante often finds himself embroiled in these conspiracies and must unravel the truth behind them.
- Facing Personal Demons: Dante's internal struggles, including his desire to avenge his mother's death and his complicated relationship with his brother Vergil, are recurring themes.
- Exploring His Own Heritage: His mixed heritage as a half-demon/half-human plays a significant role in his life. He must grapple with the implications of his lineage, his father's legacy, and his own identity, all of which pose unique challenges for him.
- Defending Humanity: Dante's overarching goal is to protect humanity from demonic threats. This duty often requires him to make difficult choices and sacrifices to ensure the safety of innocent people, adding a moral dimension to his challenges.
- Mastering New Weapons and Abilities: Throughout his life, he gains access to various weapons and devil powers. Learning to master and use these new abilities effectively in combat is a continuous challenge.
- Boss Battles: Dante frequently engages in epic confrontations with gigantic and powerful adversaries that require precise timing, strategy, and adaptability to emerge victorious.
- Adapting to New Companions and Allies: Throughout the series, he interacts with various characters, some of whom become allies. These relationships present their own set of challenges as Dante learns to trust and work alongside others who share his mission.

Overall, Dante's journey is marked by a combination of physical, emotional, and moral challenges.

PSYCHOLOGY

Dante's character in the Devil May Cry series is deeply affected by his hardships and challenges. While he maintains a confident and often cocky exterior, these challenges have significant psychological impacts on him:

- Loss and Grief: One of the central hardships Dante faces is the loss of his mother, who was killed by demons when he was a child. This traumatic event fuels his desire for revenge and is a source of deep-seated grief. Dante's quest to avenge his mother's death is a driving force in his character's psychology.
- Identity and Self-Reflection: As a half-demon, Dante grapples with questions of identity and belonging. He often questions his own humanity and struggles to come to terms with his demonic heritage. This internal conflict is a recurring theme, affecting his sense of self and self-worth.
- Family and Relationships: His complex relationship with his twin brother, Vergil, is a significant source of psychological turmoil. Vergil often represents the opposite side of the moral spectrum, seeking power at any cost, while Dante strives to protect humanity. Their conflicting ideologies and constant clashes create a deep emotional strain on him.
- Moral Dilemmas: Dante's commitment to defending humanity sometimes leads to morally complex situations. He must make difficult decisions about whether to prioritize the greater good or his personal desires. These moral dilemmas weigh on his conscience and contribute to his character development.
- Loneliness and Isolation: Despite his confident demeanor, he often finds himself isolated due to his unique abilities and the dangers he faces. This isolation can lead to feelings of loneliness and the sense that he doesn't quite fit into the human world.
- Survivor's Guilt: Dante's exceptional combat skills and his role as a demon hunter mean that he often survives battles that others do not. This can lead to feelings of guilt and survivor's remorse as he witnesses the suffering and destruction caused by demons.
- Emotional Suppression: He tends to suppress his emotions and use humor and bravado as a coping mechanism. He often hides his pain and vulnerabilities behind his tough exterior, making it

difficult for others to understand the depth of his psychological struggles.

- Post-Traumatic Stress: Constantly facing life-threatening situations and witnessing the horrors of the demon world can result in symptoms of post-traumatic stress. Dante's resilience is often tested, and he must find ways to cope with the psychological toll of his experiences.

Despite these psychological hardships, Dante remains a resilient character who continues to fight for the safety of humanity. His ability to confront his literal and figurative inner demons and his determination to protect the innocent are central aspects of his character.

OBJECT RELATIONS THEORY & DANTE

Object Relations Theory is a psychoanalytic approach that originated from the works of psychoanalysts such as Melanie Klein, Ronald Fairbairn, and D.W. Winnicott. This theory focuses on the role of interpersonal relationships, particularly early relationships with caregivers or "objects," in shaping an individual's personality and mental health. "Objects" in this context refer to people or images that become the focus of emotional investment. Applying Object Relations Theory to analyze Dante from the Devil May Cry series involves exploring how his early relationships and internalized objects may influence his character, interpersonal dynamics, and overall psychological makeup.

- Objects and Relationships: Internal and External Objects—In Object Relations Theory, the concepts of internal and external objects are fundamental to understanding how individuals form and maintain relationships. These terms refer to different aspects of an individual's psychological and emotional representations of people in his or her life.
  - External Objects: refer to the actual people, caregivers, or figures in the external world with whom an individual interacts. These are the tangible, real-life individuals who play significant roles in a person's life, especially during early development. External objects, typically primary caregivers (such as parents or caregivers in infancy), profoundly impact a person's psychological development. The nature of these early relationships

shapes the individual's perceptions, expectations, and emotional experiences.

- Internal Objects: These refer to the mental representations or images of external objects that individuals internalize through their experiences. They are the subjective, internalized versions of significant others that reside in an individual's mind. Internal objects are crucial in shaping a person's inner world and influencing their thoughts, feelings, and behaviors. These internalized representations are formed based on early interactions with external objects and continue influencing interpersonal dynamics throughout life.
- Dante's traumatic experience of losing his mother to demons at a young age shapes his early object relations. The loss of his mother and the betrayal by his father contribute to the formation of internal objects representing nurturing and threatening aspects. This early loss and betrayal may impact his ability to trust and form secure attachments. The intense emotional impact of this loss might contribute to the development of internal objects representing both nurturing (his mother) and threatening (demons) aspects. Splitting, a defense mechanism, might lead to extreme categorizations of good and evil in his worldview.
- Introjection and Projection:
  - Introjection: The process by which individuals internalize aspects of external objects, particularly caregivers. This internalization affects the formation of one's self-image and contributes to the development of internal objects.
  - Projection: Individuals may project their own feelings, desires, or qualities onto others. This process is influenced by internalized objects and can impact how individuals perceive and interact with the external world.
  - Dante's internalization of his father, Sparda, and his twin brother, Vergil, as significant objects influence his self-concept and relational dynamics. The internalized images of Sparda and Vergil may represent conflicting aspects of strength, power, and morality. Dante's internal

struggle with his demonic heritage and the legacy of his family becomes a central theme.

- Splitting Defense Mechanism: Object Relations Theory introduces the concept of splitting, where individuals may unconsciously divide their experiences and relationships into extreme opposites (e.g., good vs. bad). This splitting can impact perceptions of self and others, leading to difficulties in integrating positive and negative aspects. The concept of splitting, where individuals categorize experiences into extreme opposites (e.g., good vs. bad), is relevant to Dante's character. His internalized objects may contribute to a dualistic worldview, especially evident in his interactions with demons and the constant struggle between his demonic and human sides.

- Transitional Objects (Winnicott's Contribution): D.W. Winnicott, a key figure in Object Relations Theory, introduced the concept of transitional objects. These objects (such as a favorite blanket or toy) serve as a bridge between the child's inner world and external reality, facilitating the development of a sense of self. Dante's weapons, such as his sword Rebellion and his dual pistols Ebony and Ivory, can be seen as transitional objects in Winnicott's sense. These objects serve as symbolic bridges between his inner world and external reality, representing his identity, strength, and connection to his mission as a demon hunter.

- Object Constancy - Developmental Milestone: Object Relations Theory emphasizes the importance of achieving object constancy, where individuals can maintain a stable internal image of others even in their absence. This milestone is crucial for forming healthy and enduring relationships. Dante's ability to maintain object constancy in relationships is a relevant aspect. Object Relations Theory suggests that the stable internal representation of significant others is crucial for forming healthy and enduring connections. Examining how Dante maintains (or struggles with) object constancy in relationships, particularly with characters like Lady and Trish, can provide insights. The stable internal representation of these characters, even in their absence, is essential for forming healthy and enduring connections.

- Internal Working Models - Attachment and Relationships: Object Relations Theory contributes to our understanding of attachment by proposing that early relationships shape internal working models that guide individuals' expectations and behaviors in later relationships. Secure or insecure attachment patterns are influenced by early object relationships.
- Transference and Countertransference—Therapeutic Dynamics: Object Relations Theory is often applied in psychotherapy. Transference refers to the client's projection of feelings onto the therapist, and countertransference involves the therapist's emotional reactions. These dynamics offer insights into the client's internal objects and relational patterns.
- Pathological Object Relations - Impact on Mental Health: Disturbances in early object relationships are believed to contribute to various mental health issues. Object Relations Theory provides a framework for understanding how difficulties in forming and maintaining healthy relationships can lead to psychological challenges.
- Psychoanalytic Treatment: Object Relations Theory is often utilized in psychoanalytic treatment to explore and understand how early object relationships influence current thoughts, feelings, and behaviors. The therapeutic process aims to help individuals modify and integrate these internal objects for improved mental health. Object Relations Theory allows for exploring how disturbances in Dante's early object relations contribute to his psychological struggles. These challenges may manifest in his internal conflicts, difficulty forming stable relationships, and the perpetual quest for identity and purpose.

Object Relations Theory provides a nuanced understanding of how early relationships contribute to the development of personality, interpersonal patterns, and psychological well-being. While rooted in psychoanalysis, its concepts have been influential in various therapeutic approaches and the broader field of psychology. Object Relations Theory offers a framework for understanding the intricacies of Dante's character development, his relationships, and the internalized objects that influence his psychological landscape throughout Devil May Cry. The interplay between external and internal objects provides insights into the complexities of his persona and the emotional themes woven into the narrative.

WOLFENSTEIN

One of the most prominent main characters in Wolfenstein is B.J. Blazkowicz. He's an American soldier and war hero during an alternate history version of World War II, where the Nazis win the war and take over the world, leading to a dystopian future. B.J. suffers a head injury during the war and spends 14 years in a coma. He wakes up to find the world under Nazi control and becomes a leader of the resistance against the oppressive regime. He sets out on a journey to take on the Nazi war machine and attempt to liberate the world from their rule. He later faces personal struggles and challenges as he fights to free his homeland from Nazi control. Blazkowicz is portrayed as a courageous and determined soldier who is willing to do whatever it takes to combat the Nazi regime and protect the world from their tyranny.

CHALLENGES

Blazkowicz faces numerous challenges and obstacles throughout his journey as he battles against the oppressive Nazi regime and strives to liberate the world from their control. Some of the key challenges he encounters include:

- Overwhelming Nazi Forces: The Nazi regime in the Wolfenstein series is depicted as highly advanced and militarized. B.J. often finds himself outnumbered and outgunned, facing well-trained soldiers, advanced technology, and massive war machines.

- Personal Struggles: Blazkowicz is not just a physical warrior; he also deals with significant personal challenges. He grapples with trauma from his past, including his upbringing in an abusive household and the horrors he witnessed during World War II. Additionally, he must cope with the burden of being a leader in the resistance movement and, later on, the challenges of becoming a father.
- Infiltration and Espionage: Many missions require B.J. to go undercover, infiltrate Nazi installations, and gather vital information. These missions are often fraught with danger, as he must maintain his cover while avoiding detection.
- Advanced Technology: The Nazi regime in the Wolfenstein series possesses advanced technology, including robotic soldiers, laser weapons, and towering war machines. B.J. must adapt and find ways to counter these technological advantages.
- Morally Ambiguous Choices: B.J. often faces morally complex decisions as he fights the Nazis. He must make choices that could have significant consequences for himself and the world, such as sparing or killing enemies, deciding the fates of captured Nazi soldiers and choosing between personal relationships and the greater good.
- Physical Challenges: B.J. is not a superhuman and suffers injuries throughout the series. He must carefully manage his health and resources, as he can be easily overwhelmed in combat.
- Resistance Unity: B.J. often works with a diverse group of resistance fighters, each with their own personalities and motivations. Building and maintaining unity within the resistance is a recurring challenge.
- Navigating Hostile Environments: B.J. confronts a variety of environments, from the devastated streets of Nazi-occupied cities to underground Nazi facilities and even the surface of Venus. Each environment presents unique challenges and dangers.

Despite these challenges, B.J. Blazkowicz remains determined and resolute in his quest to free the world from Nazi oppression. His resourcefulness, combat skills, and unwavering commitment to the resistance make him a formidable protagonist in Wolfenstein.

PSYCHOLOGY

B.J. Blazkowicz undergoes significant psychological strain throughout his journey due to the hardships and traumas he faces.

- Post-Traumatic Stress Disorder (PTSD): He has witnessed and experienced extreme violence, brutality, and loss. His experiences in combat, including the horrors of the Nazi regime, have left lasting emotional scars. He exhibits symptoms of PTSD, such as flashbacks, nightmares, and emotional numbness. His struggles with PTSD are depicted as he grapples with his traumatic past.
- Survivor's Guilt: B.J. often feels guilty for surviving when others did not. This survivor's guilt weighs heavily on him and contributes to his internal emotional turmoil. He frequently reflects on the sacrifices made by his comrades and the innocent lives lost during the Nazi regime's reign.
- Personal Relationships: B.J.'s involvement in the resistance movement and his role as a leader strain his personal relationships. He worries about the safety of his loved ones and often has to make difficult decisions that affect them. Balancing his responsibilities as a father and husband with his duty to the resistance adds to his psychological burden.
- Moral Dilemmas: B.J. faces numerous moral dilemmas throughout his journey. He must make choices that challenge his sense of morality, such as whether to spare or kill enemies, decide the fate of captured Nazis, and make sacrifices for the greater good. These decisions weigh on his conscience and impact his mental well-being.
- Identity and Purpose: As the Nazi regime transforms the world, B.J. questions his identity and purpose. He must grapple with the existential crisis of being a soldier in a world that has fundamentally changed. His struggle to find meaning and purpose in the face of overwhelming adversity adds to his psychological complexity.
- Resilience and Determination: Despite the psychological toll of his experiences, B.J. demonstrates remarkable resilience and determination. He pushes through his trauma and emotional struggles to continue the fight against the Nazis. His unwavering

commitment to the resistance and the liberation of the world serves as a testament to his strength of character.

- Emotional Depth: B.J. is a multifaceted character who grapples with fear, anger, love, and despair.

Throughout Wolfenstein, Blazkowicz's psychological struggles are a central theme, and they contribute to the depth and emotional resonance.

MORAL DEVELOPMENT THEORY & B.J.

Moral Development Theory, most notably proposed by Lawrence Kohlberg, is a psychological framework that seeks to understand how individuals develop their moral reasoning and ethical decision-making abilities over time. Kohlberg's theory consists of several stages, each building upon the previous one, as individuals progress through moral dilemmas and develop more complex moral reasoning. It is important to note that not everyone reaches the highest stages of moral development, and progression through the stages is not strictly tied to age. Factors such as education, life experiences and exposure to moral dilemmas can influence moral development. The stages are more reflective of cognitive and moral maturity. Additionally, individuals may exhibit different levels of moral reasoning in different areas of their lives. Here's an overview of Kohlberg's stages of moral development:

- Pre-Conventional Level:
    - Stage 1: Obedience and Punishment Orientation (Infancy to early childhood) - At this stage, individuals focus on avoiding punishment and obeying authority figures. In the early stages of B.J.'s journey, especially during the war, he may exhibit characteristics of Stage 1. He focuses on following orders, survival, and avoiding punishment. The wartime context emphasizes the necessity of discipline and obedience.
    - Stage 2: Individualism and Exchange (Early childhood to pre-adolescence) - Here, individuals consider their own interests and understand that different people have different needs, so they engage in reciprocity. As B.J. faces the harsh realities of war and oppression, he may progress to Stage 2. He demonstrates an understanding of individual interests and engages in reciprocity, forming

alliances with fellow resistance fighters based on shared goals and mutual benefit.

- Conventional Level:
  - Stage 3: Interpersonal Relationships (Adolescence) - This stage involves a concern for maintaining social norms and gaining approval from others. Moral decisions are made based on societal expectations. B.J.'s leadership role in the resistance movement and his interactions with other characters reflect Stage 3. His decisions might be influenced by a concern for maintaining positive relationships, loyalty, and approval within the group. The bonds formed with resistance members become crucial.
  - Stage 4: Maintaining Social Order (Adolescence to adulthood) - Individuals in this stage prioritize the functioning of society and obeying laws. They value authority and social order. As B.J. assumes a leadership position, he may exhibit characteristics of Stage 4. His decisions prioritize maintaining social order within the resistance. Following rules and upholding the values of the group become essential for the functioning and success of the resistance movement.
- Post-Conventional Level:
  - Stage 5: Social Contract and Individual Rights (Adulthood) - At this stage, individuals recognize that moral rules are not fixed but can be changed for the greater good. They emphasize democratic decision-making and individual rights. In facing the atrocities of the Nazi regime and making complex moral decisions, B.J. may move toward Stage 5. His moral reasoning could involve considerations of individual rights, democratic decision-making, and a recognition that moral rules can be adapted for the greater good.
  - Stage 6: Universal Principles (Adulthood) - In the final stage, individuals operate based on universal ethical principles, such as justice, equality, and human rights. They may disobey laws that conflict with these principles. B.J.'s highest moral development may align with Stage 6, where he operates based on universal ethical principles. His decisions could be guided by a commitment to

justice, equality, and human rights. B.J.'s actions may transcend societal norms, reflecting a deep internalization of moral principles.

Analyzing B.J. Blazkowicz's character through all six stages of Lawrence Kohlberg's Moral Development Theory provides insight into his evolving moral reasoning throughout his journey. While specific actions may not perfectly align with each stage, we can make general observations based on his decisions and motivations.

THE WALKING DEAD

One of the main characters in The Walking Dead is Lee Everett. He was a middle-aged professor of history before the outbreak of a zombie apocalypse. Lee finds himself amid chaos and danger when the zombie outbreak occurs. He is initially handcuffed in the back of a police car, being transported to prison for a crime he committed before the outbreak. However, the car crashes and Lee manages to escape. He soon encounters a young girl named Clementine, whose parents are missing, and takes it upon himself to protect and care for her in this harsh new world. Lee forms relationships with other survivors, and through his decisions, he encounters morally complex choices in the face of dire circumstances.

CHALLENGES

Lee Everett faces numerous challenges and obstacles as he navigates the post-apocalyptic world infested with zombies, also known as walkers, and encounters other survivors.

- Surviving Walker Threats: Walkers are a constant and ever-present threat. Lee and his group must be vigilant and resourceful to avoid getting bitten or overwhelmed by hordes of zombies.
- Limited Resources: Food, water, and other essential supplies are scarce. Lee's group must scavenge for resources, often leading to

difficult choices about what to take and leave behind. Managing these limited resources is crucial for survival.

- Moral Dilemmas: Lee is often faced with difficult decisions that impact the lives of other survivors. These choices can be emotionally challenging and have far-reaching consequences, affecting the group dynamics and future.
- Conflict Among Survivors: The group dynamics are fragile, and tensions arise as different personalities clash. Lee must mediate conflicts and make decisions that can strengthen or weaken the group's cohesion.
- Finding Safe Shelter: Securing a safe place to stay is a constant challenge. Lee and his group must search for locations that are defensible against walkers and other hostile survivors. Finding such shelter often involves exploring abandoned buildings and making them secure.
- Dealing with Other Survivors: Not all survivors are friendly. Lee's group encounters other humans who may pose a threat through violence or deception. Deciding how to interact with these groups is a recurring challenge.
- Caring for Clementine: One of Lee's primary responsibilities is protecting and caring for Clementine, a young girl who becomes like a daughter to him. Keeping her safe and helping her navigate the world's harsh realities is a constant challenge.
- Personal Demons and Past Mistakes: Lee himself carries emotional baggage from his past, including a crime he committed before the outbreak. Dealing with his personal demons and facing the consequences of his actions is an ongoing challenge for him.
- Losing Group Members: Lee's group members may die or leave based on his decisions, leading to emotional turmoil and affecting the group's dynamics.

PSYCHOLOGY

The Walking Dead explores the psychological toll of survival in a world where the norms of society have collapsed. Lee's responses to these challenges are a central aspect, and the hardships and challenges he faces profoundly impact his psychology and emotional well-being.

- Post-Traumatic Stress: The constant threat of walkers, the loss of loved ones, and the need to make morally complex decisions can lead to severe post-traumatic stress among the survivors. They may experience nightmares, flashbacks, and a general sense of anxiety and unease.
- Guilt and Regret: Lee feels guilty and regretful about his past actions and the consequences of his decisions in the post-apocalyptic world. This guilt can weigh heavily on his mind and affect his decision-making.
- Desensitization: Surviving in a world overrun by walkers and encountering violence and death daily can desensitize to some extent. Lee may become more accustomed to acts of brutality and struggle to maintain his humanity.
- Loss of Trust: Trust is a fragile commodity in a world where betrayal and deception can lead to dire consequences. Lee may become increasingly distrustful of others, even within his own group, leading to strained relationships.
- Isolation and Loneliness: The isolation caused by the collapse of society and the loss of loved ones can lead to feelings of loneliness and despair. He grapples with the emotional toll of being cut off from the world he once knew.
- Parental Instincts: Responsible for the care of Clementine, he experiences heightened stress and anxiety. He is constantly concerned about the child's safety and well-being, leading to a strong sense of responsibility.
- Survivor's Guilt: Like those who have lost friends or family members, he too struggles with survivor's guilt, feeling guilty for being alive when others have perished.
- Loss of Empathy: In order to survive, he must make morally questionable decisions or become less empathetic towards others. This loss of empathy can be a coping mechanism but also a source of internal conflict.
- Adaptive Behaviors: Lee develops adaptive behaviors and coping mechanisms to deal with the stress and challenges of the post-apocalyptic world. These can include emotional detachment, a focus on self-preservation, and an inclination to avoid forming close attachments.
- Hope vs. Hopelessness: Lee may wrestle with maintaining hope for a better future while facing the seemingly insurmountable

odds of the zombie apocalypse. This internal struggle between hope and hopelessness can be emotionally taxing.

TRAUMA INFORMED CARE MODEL & LEE

The Trauma-Informed Care (TIC) model is an approach to understanding and responding to individuals who have experienced trauma. It emphasizes recognizing the widespread impact of trauma, understanding how it can affect an individual's mental and emotional well-being, and integrating this understanding into all aspects of care and support. Analyzing Lee Everett from The Walking Dead through a Trauma-Informed lens can provide insights into how he copes with and is affected by the traumatic events of the post-apocalyptic world.

Here are key principles of Trauma-Informed Care and how they can be applied to analyzing Lee's character:

- Safety: Creating a safe environment is foundational to Trauma-Informed Care. This involves physical and emotional safety, ensuring individuals feel secure in their surroundings and relationships. In a therapeutic or caregiving context, practitioners prioritize establishing safety to build trust with trauma survivors. This may involve setting clear boundaries, communicating openly, and creating spaces where individuals feel protected. Lee constantly strives to ensure Clementine's and his safety in a world overrun by walkers. His decisions and actions often revolve around assessing and mitigating risks to maintain their physical and emotional safety.

- Trustworthiness and Transparency: Trust is crucial for individuals who have experienced trauma. Trustworthiness and transparency involve building trust through honesty, reliability, and consistency in interactions. Practitioners or caregivers must be reliable and transparent in their actions and communication. Clear and honest information helps survivors feel secure and fosters a sense of trust in the relationship. Lee's interactions with other survivors reflect the importance of trust. He must decide whom to trust and whom to be cautious of, as betrayal and deception are common in the post-apocalyptic world.

- Peer Support and Connection: Recognizing the importance of social connections and support networks in promoting healing and resilience. Encouraging individuals to connect with supportive peers or groups can be integral to Trauma-Informed Care. Group therapy, support groups, or peer mentoring programs are examples of fostering connection. Lee forms connections with various survivors throughout the game, providing emotional support to one another in the face of trauma and adversity. His paternal bond with Clementine is a prime example of the importance of connection.

- Empowerment and Choice: Empowering individuals by involving them in decision-making and providing choices that allow them to have agency in their lives. Practitioners strive to involve survivors in decisions related to their care, respecting their autonomy and preferences. Empowering choices contribute to a sense of control and self-efficacy. Lee's character demonstrates this principle as he often faces morally complex decisions, and his choices directly impact the future. Even in dire circumstances, Lee's ability to make choices reflects his sense of empowerment.

- Cultural, Historical, and Gender Issues: This model acknowledges and respects the influence of cultural, historical, and gender-related factors on an individual's experience of trauma. Trauma-Informed Care should be culturally sensitive and aware of the historical and gender-specific aspects that may impact an individual's response to trauma. This includes recognizing and respecting diverse perspectives and experiences. While "The Walking Dead" doesn't explicitly delve into these issues, Lee's background and experiences as an African-American man could be examined in the context of how his identity may influence his responses to trauma.

- Resilience and Coping: Recognizing and fostering an individual's resilience and coping skills to navigate and overcome trauma. Trauma survivors often demonstrate resilience in various ways. Practitioners aim to identify and build on existing coping mechanisms while introducing new strategies to help individuals manage stress and adversity. Lee's character exemplifies resilience as he navigates the traumatic events, adapts to new challenges, and finds ways to cope with the emotional toll of the post-apocalyptic world.

- Avoiding Retraumatization: Ensuring that care and support are delivered in a way that avoids triggering or re-traumatizing individuals who have experienced trauma. Practitioners are cautious about the language used, the environment created, and the methods employed in therapy or care settings. This involves understanding potential triggers and working to minimize the risk of re-traumatization. Throughout his journey, while not in a therapeutic setting, Lee's character is marked by his past actions and guilt, and is presented with choices that force him to confront his past and potentially experience re-traumatization. In a therapeutic setting, this is something that has to be avoided.

Implementing Trauma-Informed Care involves a holistic approach that considers the unique needs and experiences of trauma survivors. It emphasizes creating a supportive and empowering environment that respects individual autonomy and fosters resilience and healing. Analyzing Lee through the Trauma-Informed Care model underscores the profound impact of trauma on his character and his responses to the post-apocalyptic world. His actions, relationships, and decision-making reflect the principles of creating safety, fostering trust, and recognizing the importance of connection and empowerment in the face of trauma. Additionally, it highlights how Lee's experiences, including his role as a caregiver to Clementine, are shaped by the traumatic events and challenges he encounters.

MAX PAYNE

In Max Payne (Remedy Entertainment | Rockstar Games), the main character is, unsurprisingly, Max Payne himself. He is a former New York City police detective who becomes a vigilante after a series of tragic events in his life. Max's life takes a dark turn when his wife and daughter are brutally murdered by a group of drug addicts high on a mysterious new drug called Valkyr. Max becomes addicted to painkillers and goes on a relentless quest for revenge against those responsible for his family's death. He also uncovers a vast conspiracy involving the drug trade within the city's criminal underworld. Max is once again thrust into a complex web of conspiracies and betrayal when he reunites with Mona Sax, a deadly assassin who may have ties to the criminal organization he's trying to bring down. After Max leaves New York, he begins working as a private security contractor in Sao Paulo, Brazil. He's battling addiction and depression while trying to protect a wealthy businessman's family from a violent gang. Max continues to descend into darkness and attempts to find some semblance of redemption. With his leather jacket and constant reliance on painkillers, Max is characterized by his internal monologues, which provide insight into his thoughts and emotions, making him a complex and compelling character dealing with vengeance, redemption, and personal demons.

CHALLENGES

Many things contribute to the intense and dark atmosphere in Max's world, and he has many challenges to overcome.

- Personal Tragedy: Payne's journey begins with a deeply personal tragedy - the brutal murder of his wife and daughter. Coping with the loss of his loved ones is a constant emotional struggle for him.
- Valkyr Drug: Max becomes embroiled in a dangerous conspiracy involving the Valkyr drug. As he investigates its origins and distribution, he must confront ruthless drug lords, corrupt police officers, and violent gang members who will stop at nothing to protect their interests.
- Betrayal and Deception: He often finds himself betrayed or deceived by people he trusts. He becomes entangled with Mona Sax, an assassin who may have her own agenda, leading to a sense of uncertainty and danger.
- Psychological Struggles: Max Payne grapples with his own inner demons, including addiction to painkillers and severe depression. His internal monologues reveal his inner turmoil.
- Physical Peril: He is frequently in mortal danger and engages in intense gunfights with hordes of enemies, often with overwhelming odds.
- Descent into Darkness: Max gradually descends into darkness as he becomes more ruthless and willing to do whatever it takes to achieve his goals. This moral conflict is a significant challenge for him.
- Redemption and Closure: He is driven by a desire for revenge but also seeks redemption and closure for the events that have haunted him. This pursuit of justice and his internal struggle to find meaning in his actions are central challenges.

Max Payne's challenges are not just physical but also psychological and emotional. His journey is one of self-discovery, redemption, and survival in a world filled with corruption, betrayal, and violence.

PSYCHOLOGY

The hardships and challenges he faces throughout his journey profoundly impact his psychology, leading to significant changes in his character and mental state.

- Grief and Loss: The murder of Max's wife and daughter is a traumatic event that leaves him emotionally scarred. His grief and an overwhelming sense of loss drive him to a state of deep depression and despair. Max's inner monologues and constant references to his family reflect his inability to move on from this tragedy.
- Addiction: He turns to painkillers as a way to cope with physical and emotional pain. His reliance on these drugs becomes an addiction, which further complicates his psychological state. The painkillers serve as a metaphor for Max's attempts to numb his emotional pain and escape from reality.
- Isolation and Loneliness: His journey is marked by isolation and loneliness. He often finds himself alienated from others due to his obsession with vengeance and his inability to connect with people on a deeper level. His internal monologues reveal a sense of detachment from the world around him.
- Ruthlessness: As Max's quest for revenge intensifies, he becomes increasingly ruthless and violent. He is willing to do whatever it takes to achieve his goals, including killing numerous enemies in brutal fashion. This transformation reflects his growing inner darkness and moral ambiguity.
- Paranoia and Betrayal: His experiences with betrayal and deception make him increasingly paranoid. He finds it difficult to trust others, and his sense of paranoia adds to his psychological distress. The blurred lines between friend and foe contribute to his constant state of tension.
- Redemption and Self-Reflection: Despite his descent into darkness, Max also experiences moments of self-reflection and a desire for redemption. He questions his own actions and seeks meaning in his pursuit of justice.
- Survivor's Guilt: He often expresses a sense of survivor's guilt, feeling responsible for the deaths of his loved ones. This guilt weighs heavily on him and contributes to his self-destructive behavior.

- Cynicism: Throughout his journey, Max becomes increasingly cynical about the world and the people in it. He sees corruption and moral decay everywhere, and this cynicism further isolates him from society.

Max Payne's psychology undergoes a profound transformation as he grapples with grief, addiction, isolation, and a relentless pursuit of vengeance. The hardships and challenges he faces push him to the brink of his sanity, resulting in a complex and distraught man.

COGNITIVE BEHAVIORAL MODEL & MAX PAYNE

The Cognitive-Behavioral Model (CBT) is a widely used and effective approach in psychology and psychotherapy that focuses on the interplay between a person's thoughts, feelings, and behaviors. It is rooted in the idea that our thoughts and beliefs about ourselves, others, and the world around us significantly influence our emotions and actions. CBT aims to identify and change negative thought patterns and behaviors to improve emotional well-being and overall functioning. Here are the key components of the CBT model:

- Cognition (Thoughts): At the core of CBT is the understanding that our thoughts and beliefs shape our emotional responses. These thoughts can be either rational or irrational. Rational thoughts are based on evidence, reason, and objective reality. Irrational thoughts are distorted, biased, or unrealistic beliefs that can lead to emotional distress. Max Payne is plagued by negative thought patterns, often engaging in self-criticism and catastrophizing. His constant internal monologues reflect his pessimism and cynicism about the world. For example, Max's recurring thoughts about his inability to protect his family contribute to feelings of guilt and despair.

- Emotion (Feelings): Emotions are the natural responses we experience based on our thoughts and interpretations of events or situations. CBT acknowledges that emotions are not inherently good or bad but simply responses to our thoughts. Emotional distress often results from negative or irrational thinking patterns. Max's negative thought patterns give rise to intense emotional distress. He experiences profound grief, anger, guilt, and depression as a result of his traumatic experiences. His grief over the loss of his wife and daughter is compounded by his belief that he failed to save them.

- Behavior (Actions): Our thoughts and emotions influence our behaviors. How we feel about a situation can determine how we act in response to it. Problematic behaviors may develop as coping mechanisms for dealing with distressing thoughts and emotions. Max's emotional distress often leads to maladaptive behaviors. He turns to alcohol and becomes addicted to painkillers as a means to cope with his emotional and physical pain. Max's reliance on painkillers is a behavior that provides temporary relief from his suffering but ultimately exacerbates his problems.
- Cognitive Distortions: CBT identifies various cognitive distortions or thinking errors that can contribute to emotional distress. Common distortions include:
    - All-or-nothing thinking: Seeing things in black-and-white terms with no middle ground.
    - Catastrophizing: Expecting the worst possible outcome.
    - Personalization: Assuming that everything is about oneself.
    - Overgeneralization: Drawing sweeping conclusions based on limited evidence.
    - Mind reading: Believing you know what others are thinking.
    - Should statements: Imposing unrealistic expectations on oneself or others.

Max exhibits cognitive distortions, such as black-and-white thinking and personalization. He often blames himself for events beyond his control and views the world in starkly negative terms. To escape from his emotional pain, he engages in avoidance behaviors. He isolates himself from others, avoids forming meaningful connections, and seeks dangerous situations as a form of distraction.

- Behavioral Strategies: CBT employs various behavioral strategies to address maladaptive behaviors and develop healthier ones. These may include:
    - Exposure therapy: Gradual and controlled exposure to feared or avoided situations.

- Behavioral experiments: Testing the validity of irrational beliefs through behavioral actions.
    - Activity scheduling: Structuring daily routines to promote positive behaviors.
    - Relaxation techniques: Teaching relaxation and stress-reduction methods.

Max could benefit from developing healthier coping mechanisms to replace his reliance on alcohol and painkillers. Therapy might involve teaching him relaxation techniques, stress management, and problem-solving skills. He could learn healthier ways to manage his emotional pain, such as through mindfulness meditation or exercise.

- Cognitive Restructuring: Central to CBT is cognitive restructuring, which involves identifying and challenging irrational or negative thought patterns. Through questioning and evidence-based analysis, individuals learn to replace irrational thoughts with more rational and balanced ones. In a CBT framework, therapy would involve helping Max identify and challenge his cognitive distortions. Therapists might encourage him to reframe his negative thoughts and develop more balanced and realistic beliefs. For example, Max could work on understanding that he couldn't control the actions of his family's killers and that his self-blame is based on distorted thinking.
- Homework and Self-Monitoring: CBT often includes homework assignments and self-monitoring tasks to help individuals practice new skills and track their progress. Keeping thought records or journals can help identify and modify thought patterns. Given Max's penchant for seeking out dangerous situations, exposure therapy could be used to address his tendency for self-destructive behavior. This therapy involves gradually exposing the individual to feared or avoided situations in a controlled and therapeutic manner. He could work with a therapist to confront his fear of vulnerability and loss by gradually opening up to others and forming meaningful connections.
- Goal-Oriented and Time-Limited: CBT is typically goal-oriented and time-limited, with specific objectives for therapy established early on. The therapist and client collaborate to set achievable goals and work systematically toward them.

CBT has been widely applied to treat various psychological conditions, including depression, anxiety disorders, phobias, post-traumatic stress disorder (PTSD), and many others. It is valued for its structured and evidence-based approach and its focus on empowering individuals to develop practical skills for managing their thoughts, emotions, and behaviors. A therapeutic approach based on CBT principles could help Max challenge these patterns and develop healthier ways of coping with his traumatic experiences and inner demons.

THE SIMS

"The Sims" is a popular life simulation (Maxis | Electronic Arts) that doesn't have a single overarching storyline but instead offers open-ended gameplay that allows players to create and control virtual people, known as "Sims," and guide them through various aspects of their lives. The main focus is to manage the daily lives of these Sims, including their needs, relationships, careers, and aspirations. Each player chooses what is most important to them and how to evolve their Sim to reach that goal. Here's a general overview of the Sims and features that have been consistent throughout the series **and my unfiltered thoughts in bold**:

- Character Creation: Players start by creating one or more Sims and customizing their appearance, personality traits, and aspirations. Each Sim has unique characteristics and desires. **Think of it like the genes you were born with, the personality you have, the clothes you buy, and the haircut you maintain (and sometimes change if you're brave enough for that).**
- Building and Furnishing: Players can build and customize homes for their Sims, choosing from a wide range of architectural styles and decorating options. They can also purchase and place furniture and other items to make their Sim's living space unique. **Do you have style? Have you stylized your home? What does it look like?**
- Needs and Aspirations: Sims have basic needs, such as hunger, hygiene, social interaction, and entertainment. Players must

manage these needs to keep their Sims happy and healthy. Additionally, Sims have long-term aspirations that players can work towards to fulfill their life goals. **Do you have long-term aspirations? What are your life goals?**

- Relationships: Players can control the interactions between Sims, allowing them to form friendships, romantic relationships, or even engage in conflicts. Relationships can impact a Sim's overall happiness and well-being. **Mmmm, this is sometimes a hard one. There's a family that you need (and want) to be present for. There are friends - the family you have chosen. Then there are romantic relationships - they come and go, and hopefully, one day, you find one that stays and fulfills you.**
- Career and Skills: Sims can pursue various careers and develop skills in areas like cooking, painting, music, and more. Advancing in their careers and mastering skills can lead to improved job opportunities and income. **What do you like to do? What do you want to do better? How can you improve your career? Will it make you happy?**
- Life Stages: Sims progress through different life stages, including babies, children, teenagers, adults, and eventually seniors. Each life stage brings its own set of challenges and opportunities. **We all get older (hopefully); we can't avoid it at all.**
- Open-Ended Gameplay: The beauty of The Sims is that there is no fixed storyline or end goal. Players can create their narratives and make choices that impact their Sims' lives, leading to endless possibilities and outcomes. **Well, isn't this like real life?**

While The Sims doesn't have a linear storyline, it provides players with a sandbox environment where they can shape the lives of their virtual characters and create their own stories, which is a significant part of its enduring appeal.

CHALLENGES

In The Sims, players face various challenges as they manage the lives of their virtual Sims. While it is open-ended and doesn't have a traditional narrative with specific challenges to overcome, there are several common challenges and goals that players can encounter:

- Meeting Sims' Needs: Sims have a set of basic needs, including hunger, hygiene, social interaction, entertainment, and more.

Players must ensure that their Sims' needs are met to keep them happy and healthy. Balancing these needs can be challenging, especially as Sims have varying preferences and schedules. **I get it. I get them. My body keeps needing stuff like food and showers. Nobody likes it when I'm hangry.**

- Career Advancement: Sims can choose from various careers, and players are tasked with helping them advance in their chosen fields. This involves improving job performance, attending work regularly, and managing the job's demands to earn promotions and higher salaries. **So much commitment. I have to continually show up at work in order to advance and earn promotions. When does it ever end?**

- Skill Development: Sims can acquire skills in areas like cooking, painting, gardening, and more. Players often set goals to improve these skills, which can lead to new job opportunities, hobbies, and income streams. **Personally, this is my favorite part of life. Learning new things that interest me and getting better at them.**

- Relationship Management: Building and maintaining relationships with other Sims is a key aspect. Players must navigate the complexities of friendships, romantic relationships, and family dynamics, all while considering the personalities and desires of each Sim. **Embracing Family members? Getting to know other people and falling in love? This might be tricky - but isn't this what we live for?**

- Financial Management: Players need to manage the finances of their Sims, which includes paying bills, purchasing necessities, and saving for future investments, like home upgrades. **Where is the "Rosebud" code in real life?**

- Family Dynamics: Players may choose to create and manage families with multiple Sims, each with their own needs and desires. Balancing the needs and aspirations of family members can be challenging. **Yes... taking into account other people's needs and sometimes giving up or settling on your own is always tough. But it is better with them in your life.**

- Time Management: Time passes in The Sims, and players must plan their Sims' daily activities to maximize productivity and happiness. Balancing work, social life, and leisure time can be a juggling act. **Don't they just use Google Calendar? Made my life way easier to track.**

- Random Events: There are random events that can disrupt a Sim's life, such as fires, burglaries, and alien abductions. Players must respond to these events quickly to minimize their impact. **Sometimes these events in life suck (did anyone say war?), and sometimes, they open doors to new possibilities. I guess that's part of life.**

- Exploration and Creativity: Part of the fun in The Sims is exploring vast customization options. Players often challenge themselves to create unique homes, Sims, and stories, pushing the boundaries of their creativity. **This is what I live for!**

It's important to note that The Sims is designed to be a flexible and player-driven experience. The challenges and goals a player encounters can vary greatly depending on their playstyle and the goals they set for themselves. Whether players are focused on building the perfect family, achieving career success, or pursuing creative endeavors, The Sims offers various challenges and opportunities for personal expression. **Like life - what are you focused on at the moment? Is that your goal in The Sims, too?**

PSYCHOLOGY

The players' choices in The Sims can significantly impact the psychology and emotional well-being of their characters (Sims). The mechanics are designed to simulate the emotional responses of Sims to various situations and interactions. Here's how player choices can affect the psychology of their Sims:

- Emotions: Sims experience many emotions, including happiness, sadness, anger, and more. Player choices and interactions with other Sims can trigger these emotions. For example, a friendly conversation can make a Sim happy, while a negative social interaction can lead to anger or sadness. **How can you make sure you're always with great emotions? I keep reminding myself that there is no good without the bad. It's tricky trying to remind yourself that through the bad moods.**

- Moodlets: There are "moodlets" to represent a Sim's current emotional state. These small icons and descriptions appear above a Sim's head and provide insight into their feelings.

Positive actions, like achieving a personal goal or having a pleasant social interaction, can result in positive moodlets. At the same time, negative experiences, such as failure or humiliation, can lead to negative moodlets. **I just use my face.**

- Long-Term Effects: Repeated positive or negative experiences can have long-term effects on a Sim's personality and behavior. For example, a Sim who experiences frequent social rejection may become more socially anxious or introverted over time. Conversely, a Sim who enjoys a successful career may develop a confident and ambitious personality. **I guess the trick is trying little things bit by bit until you receive the right feedback and experience and then trying a bit more. The key is not giving up.**

- Relationships: Player choices in interactions with other Sims can strengthen or weaken relationships. Building positive relationships with family members, friends, or romantic partners can boost a Sim's emotional well-being. On the other hand, betrayals, conflicts, or neglect can lead to strained relationships and negative emotions. **We all need to mind our relationships.**

- Aspirations: Each Sim has a set of aspirations that represent their life goals and desires. Players can choose which aspirations to pursue for their Sims, and achieving milestones related to these aspirations can bring a sense of fulfillment and happiness to the Sim. **Aspirations are cool, but you actually need to do something to fulfill them.**

- Personality Traits: Players assign personality traits to their Sims during character creation. These traits can influence how Sims reacts to different situations and interactions. For example, a "hot-headed" Sim may be more prone to anger, while a "cheerful" Sim may be more easily lifted out of negative emotions. **Choose wisely! These can be hard to change.**

- Autonomy vs. Player Control: The Sims allows players to control their Sims' actions directly or let them make decisions autonomously. Players can influence their Sims' emotions and psychology through direct actions or by setting guidelines for their behavior and watching how they respond to various situations on their own. **In life - this is deciding if you lay low and let things happen to you.... Or if you are going to make things happen for yourself.**

- Life Events: Significant life events, such as marriages, childbirth, promotions, and even deaths, can profoundly affect a Sim's emotional state and psychology. Players must navigate these events and provide support and care to their Sims accordingly. **Yep.**

Overall, The Sims' intricate simulation mechanics aim to make the virtual characters feel more lifelike by allowing their emotions and psychological states to respond dynamically to the player's choices and world. This adds depth and encourages players to consider their Sims' emotional well-being and happiness as they make decisions and guide their virtual lives.

HOW CAN YOU BECOME A BETTER SIMS PLAYER?

OR... HOW CAN YOU BECOME BETTER AT LIFE?

Becoming a better player involves mastering various aspects of the game (life), from managing the needs of your Sims (yourself) to creating engaging stories and environments. Here are some tips to help you improve your skills and enjoy a more rewarding gameplay (life) experience:

- Learn the Basics: Start by understanding the fundamental mechanics of the game, including Sim needs, interactions, and controls. Explore the game's tutorials and help menus to get a grasp of the basics.

  Learn as much as you can about life, social interactions, career paths and connect to your inner-self. You can use everything you've learned so far, the people surrounding you and the internet to learn and grasp the basics.

- Set Goals and Challenges: Establish clear objectives for your Sims or your gameplay. This could involve achieving certain career milestones, building a dream home, or creating a multi-generational legacy.

  Think about what you want in life and set mini goals to achieve it. Is it career goals? Relationships? Travel? Build your own home? You can do it all - if you plan it!

- Manage Sim Needs Efficiently: Prioritize and manage your Sims' needs effectively to keep them happy and healthy. Use time management wisely to balance work, relationships, and personal development with meeting needs.

Manage your needs efficiently. Make sure you take care of yourself mentally and physically. If you're constantly tired or not eating well, you won't be able to achieve anything else. Manage your time wisely to balance work, relationships and personal development to achieve your goals. You also need downtime to charge!

- Learn About Traits and Aspirations: Familiarize yourself with the various personality traits and aspirations. Choose traits and aspirations that align with your goals and desired storyline.

Life is a constant journey of self-improvement. You can change any trait that you think is holding you back. Just notice people around you who possess the traits you want and try to copy them. Try it slowly and see how the environment reacts.

- Experiment and Explore: Don't be afraid to experiment with different Sims, careers, and gameplay styles to find what suits you best.

Live life like you want to. You can have your own goals, and you don't need to live by someone else's standards. Do what makes you happy and continue developing. One person will only be happy if they've made it in their career, and another person will be happy if they can be self-reliant, grow their own vegetables, or travel the world without owning a thing. You do you.

- Master Skills: Focus on developing specific skills that align with your Sims' aspirations or interests. Maxing out skills can lead to better job opportunities and open up new interactions and hobbies.

This tip is not for everyone—you don't need to master all the skills in your chosen path—but if there is something that interests you and you want to improve at, why not? Do it for yourself!

- Build and Decorate Creatively: Experiment with home building and interior design. There are plenty of tutorials and guides available online to help you improve your architectural and decorating skills.

Make your home feel like you want it to. Home is where the heart is, and it is your place to relax and recharge. Make it feel right for you, even if you're a nomad. Find the way.

- Understand Relationships: Learn how to build and maintain positive relationships between Sims. Explore different romantic and social interactions to strengthen bonds or resolve conflicts. **This is important. We humans are social creatures. We need to love and feel loved. While we don't necessarily need to have a lot of friends and family - we do need quality connections. You can't have that without putting yourself out there - taking interest in others and making yourself vulnerable. We better ourselves and evolve with relationships.**

- Practice Patience and Adaptability: Understand that Sims can sometimes have a mind of their own. Be patient and adaptable when unexpected events or situations arise. Embrace the game's unpredictability, as it often leads to unique and memorable moments.

  Be patient. Embrace the unpredictability of life, as it often leads to unique and memorable moments. Becoming better at life is a journey that involves learning, experimenting and enjoying the freedom that the life you 'drew in the raffle' has to offer. There are endless opportunities to make your life more enjoyable and fulfilling.

AN ENDING NOTE

While it's true that these characters face numerous challenges and hardships in their adventures, it's essential to remember that the world of video games is a fictional realm designed for entertainment. Each person's journey is unique, and comparing our lives to fictional characters can be unproductive. Instead of dwelling on the hardships of others, it's often more beneficial to focus on our own goals, aspirations, and challenges. Every individual encounters their own set of obstacles and opportunities, and the key to personal growth and fulfillment lies in how we navigate and overcome these challenges. So, let's embrace our real-life adventures, work toward our goals, and appreciate the richness of our own experiences.

While writing this, I made sure to write the character's name as doing all of these amazing feats... but if you've played any of these games (and hopefully more than one) - the one who has actually beaten these odds... the one who has actually gone through these challenges - was you! You took the time to try. You took the time to figure it out... to go through many puzzles and tasks while keeping a clear head and working towards the goals. It was you! And if you can do it in an effing video game... you can do it in "real" life.

REFERENCES

BOOKS & MAGAZINES

- Pichère, P., & Cadiat, A.-C. (2015). *Maslow's hierarchy of needs*. Lemaitre.
- Maslow, A. H. (1943). A theory of human motivation. *Psychological Review, 50*(4), 370–396.
- Erikson, Erik H. The Life Cycle Completed. Extended version. New York: Norton, 1998. Print.
- Ryan, R. M., & Deci, E. L. (2000). Self-determination theory and the facilitation of intrinsic motivation, social development, and well-being. American Psychologist, 55, 68-78.
- Folkman, S., & Lazarus, R. S. (1985). If it changes, it must be a process: Study of emotion and coping during three stages of a college examination. *Journal of Personality and Social Psychology, 48*, 150–170.
- Borrell-Carrió, F.; Suchman, A.L. and Epstein, R.M. (2004) 'The Biopsychosocial Model 25 Years Later: Principles, Practice, and Scientific Inquiry' *Annals of Family Medicine* 2(6):576–582.
- Sandler, J., Holder, A., Dare, C., & Dreher, A. U. (1999). Freud's models of the mind *Psychoanalytic Psychology, 16*(3), 477–480.
- Lazarus, R. S. (1961). Freud's Psychoanalytic Theory of Personality. In R. S. Lazarus, *Adjustment and personality* (pp. 137–163). McGraw-Hill Book Company.
- Bearden, S. R., Cox, M. J., & Freilinger, K. (2008). Jungian theory and therapy. In K. Jordan (Ed.), *The quick theory reference guide: A resource for expert and novice mental health professionals* (pp. 31–46). Nova Science Publishers.
- Jung, C. G. (Carl Gustav), 1875-1961. The Archetypes and the Collective Unconscious. [Princeton, N.J.] :Princeton University Press, 1980.
- Myers, I. B. (1962). *The Myers-Briggs Type Indicator: Manual (1962)*. Consulting Psychologists Press.
- McCrae, R. R., & Costa, P. T., Jr. (2008). The five-factor theory of personality. In O. P. John, R. W. Robins, & L. A. Pervin (Eds.), *Handbook of personality: Theory and research* (3rd ed., pp. 159–181). The Guilford Press.
- Eysenck, H. J. (1990). Biological dimensions of personality. In L. A. Pervin (Ed.), *Handbook of personality: Theory and research* (pp. 244–276). The Guilford Press.

- Schneider, K. J., Pierson, J. F., & Bugental, J. F. T. (Eds.). (2015). *The handbook of humanistic psychology: Theory, research, and practice* (2nd ed.). Sage Publications, Inc.
- Bretherton, I. (1992). The origins of attachment theory: John Bowlby and Mary Ainsworth. *Developmental Psychology, 28*(5), 759–775.
- Seligman, M. E. P., & Csikszentmihalyi, M. (2000). Positive psychology: An introduction. *American Psychologist, 55*(1), 5–14.
- Bandura, A., & National Inst of Mental Health. (1986). *Social foundations of thought and action: A social cognitive theory.* Prentice-Hall, Inc.
- Bandura, A. (1977). *Social learning theory.* Prentice-Hall.
- Frankl, Viktor E. (Viktor Emil), 1905-1997, author. Man's Search for Meaning : an Introduction to Logotherapy. Boston :Beacon Press, 1962.
- Ehlers, A., & Clark, D. M. (2000). A cognitive model of posttraumatic stress disorder. *Behaviour Research and Therapy, 38*(4), 319–345.
- Fairbairn, W. R. D. (1954). *An object-relations theory of the personality.* Basic Books.
- Buttell, F. P., & Carney, M. M. (2008). Moral development theory. In B. A. Thyer, K. M. Sowers, & C. N. Dulmus (Eds.), *Comprehensive handbook of social work and social welfare, Vol. 2. Human behavior in the social environment* (pp. 379–395). John Wiley & Sons Inc.
- Classen, C. C., & Clark, C. S. (2017). Trauma-informed care. In S. N. Gold (Ed.), *APA handbook of trauma psychology: Trauma practice* (pp. 515–541). American Psychological Association.
- Hupp, S. D. A., Reitman, D., & Jewell, J. D. (2008). Cognitive-behavioral theory. In M. Hersen & A. M. Gross (Eds.), *Handbook of clinical psychology, Vol. 2. Children and adolescents* (pp. 263–287). John Wiley & Sons, Inc..

WEBSITES

- https://mario.nintendo.com/history/
- https://zelda.fandom.com/wiki/Zelda_Timeline
- https://www.simplypsychology.org/Erik-Erikson.html
- https://half-life.fandom.com/wiki/Portal_storyline
- https://half-life.fandom.com/wiki/Half-Life_storyline
- https://bioshock.fandom.com/wiki/BioShock
- https://nightinthewoods.fandom.com/wiki/Night_in_the_Woods
- https://heavyrain.fandom.com/wiki/Heavy_Rain
- https://godofwar.fandom.com/wiki/God_of_War_(2018)
- https://silenthill.fandom.com/wiki/Silent_Hill_2
- https://www.dangerousdave.com/saga
- https://tombraider.fandom.com/wiki/Tomb_Raider_(Franchise)
- https://hero.fandom.com/wiki/Commander_Keen
- https://keenwiki.shikadi.net/wiki/Main_Page
- https://sonic.fandom.com/wiki/Sonic_the_Hedgehog
- https://witcher.fandom.com/wiki/The_Witcher_storyline
- https://thelastofus.fandom.com/wiki/The_Last_of_Us
- https://monkeyisland.fandom.com/wiki/The_Secret_of_Monkey_Island
- https://uncharted.fandom.com/wiki/Uncharted_Wiki:Main_Page
- https://en.wikipedia.org/wiki/Simon_the_Sorcerer_(series)
- https://residentevil.fandom.com/wiki/Resident_Evil/plot
- https://metalgear.fandom.com/wiki/Metal_Gear_Solid
- https://devilmaycry.fandom.com/wiki/Devil_May_Cry_(series)
- https://wolfenstein.fandom.com/wiki/The_Story_So_Far...
- https://telltalegames.fandom.com/wiki/The_Walking_Dead
- https://maxpayne.fandom.com/wiki/Max_Payne_(Series)
- https://sims.fandom.com/wiki/The_Sims_Wiki